TEACHING

with

ENDURANCE

*Building the resilience
to teach for the long haul*

BRAD KAHRS

AuthorHouse™
1663 Liberty Drive
Bloomington, IN 47403
www.authorhouse.com
Phone: 833-262-8899

Because of the dynamic nature of the Internet, any web addresses or links contained in this book may have changed since publication and may no longer be valid. The views expressed in this work are solely those of the author and do not necessarily reflect the views of the publisher, and the publisher hereby disclaims any responsibility for them.

Any people depicted in stock imagery provided by Getty Images are models, and such images are being used for illustrative purposes only.
Certain stock imagery © Getty Images.

This book is printed on acid-free paper.

ISBN: 978-1-6655-7674-1 (sc)
ISBN: 978-1-6655-7673-4 (e)

Library of Congress Control Number: 2022921849

Print information available on the last page.

Published by AuthorHouse 11/29/2022

Cover created by Darin Hamm

authorHOUSE

CONTENTS

FOREWORD/PROLOGUE

It's been a journey, this teacher's life. It's been an incredible "ride", filled with challenge and setbacks, frustration and discouragement, BUT it has also been filled with memories and moments, lessons and love. As I near the end of this amazing "race" I continually encounter opportunities to share something with current and future teachers alike. I want to pass on some of the good stuff to those that follow me on this adventure of the teaching life. Early in life my dad imparted the lesson that we should always leave a thing better than when we got there. This book is intended to capture the lessons and experiences of a teacher's life that is now four decades long. It is my hope that in sharing the things that I've learned, along with some personal stories of both failure and success, I can contribute something worthy to other teachers on their own journeys and thus leave the profession a little bit better than when I got here.

I must acknowledge that many of the specific ideas are not my own. I did my best to cite the source of all ideas that came from someone else. However, the stories are mine or have been shared with me during a professional conversation and just maybe these stories will illuminate what matters most with the light of a long-time practitioner. This book is not a work of art, but a work of heart written by an educator who loves to teach as much now as I did back in 1983 when I started. I was once told by an administrator that I'm too "touchy-feely." That's probably true but I know that when the heart is fully engaged then opportunities to impact a life are most accessible. I will admit that emotion without information and truth can result in a frenetic bouncing of one idea to the next, but I know that truth without emotion produces lifeless ideas. I recently encountered the following word picture: Truth and thought is the furnace, the heart and emotion is the fuel, and the teacher is the ignition. I have been fortunate to have worked with and been taught by many excellent teachers. Those teachers have ignited so much good in my life. I offer Isaac Newton's quote to capture my sincere belief that my life has been incredibly blessed by dozens of excellent teachers: *If I have seen a little further it is by standing on the shoulders of giants.*

I started writing this book as I completed a dissertation where I interviewed dozens of beginning teachers and their district-assigned mentors in an attempt to root out mentoring practices that were most effective in helping novice teachers. I continued writing as I entered Higher Ed and found myself in classrooms from kindergarten through 12th grade supporting pre-service teachers in practicum experiences. I dedicate this book to those teachers who love deeply yet struggle to hold onto the passion and purpose that makes each day an adventure. For too many educators a career can turn into a long, dark uphill climb with no end in sight. I set this work down several times. As a writer I have wrestled hard with the inner voice that whispers, "It doesn't matter." Each time I set this project aside with its vast array of "stiki" notes, index cards, journals, and printouts placed in a big box, the thought "I can't, I'm done" would echo in my head. But then something, no wait, someone, always a teacher or former student, would breathe life into my heart and soul.

I am reminded of a time, when in the mountains of Colorado with a former student, after getting lost because of heavy spring snowfalls, I ended up clinging to a cliff (and fearing for my life). His calm voice, a trusted voice, talked me down the cliff. Each movement down the death-defying climb was guided and encouraged by his voice. I ended up doing something I didn't think I could do (and living to tell about it). My love for the mountains and mountain adventures grew that day. It is my intent to provide a voice that can help you recapture the confidence and courage to continue doing great things for kids.

In the many years I've invested in the teaching profession I have failed often. Yet my pursuit of understanding combined with a love for fellow teachers has kept me "clinging to the cliff." This pursuit has allowed me to combine research and all the requirements of a scientific perspective with the experience of teaching kids of all ages and young adults that are preparing to teach kids. The emotions of this work are a vital part of building endurance. As the definition of endurance that I keep close reminds me, **endurance is more than the ability to bear a hard thing, but to turn it into glory.**" With endurance we can hold onto hope and love. I still love to sit with a student or a group of students, or practicing teachers and generate ideas, strategies, and solutions. I still hope that teaching becomes the profession that our best and brightest long for. I still hope that teachers in the United States and around the world get treated with reverence and respect and are rewarded for what they give. I still believe that we can create a Teacher Development system that helps teachers consistently recollect the pieces of their hearts that get spent and scattered in the mental, physical, and emotional toll of a teacher's life and allows them to pour more of themselves into their students. I believe that instead of battling burnout we can help teachers develop the habits and actions of endurance and provide them with the time and support that allows them to find their best and most passionate selves, over and over and over again.

During the summer of 2020 (after months of staying isolated because of COVID) I just had to escape. I went to the San Juan mountains in southwestern Colorado for some beauty and adventure. Along the way I spent a couple of days in Delta, Colorado, my hometown for over a decade. Somewhat serendipitously I was able to meet with a former student-athlete who is currently a medical student at George Washington University. At one point in the conversation, she asked me, "How can you write such perfectly meaningful messages in the cards and letters you send?" My first reaction resulted in a somewhat flippant response of "Practice, Practice, Practice." Yet, this question stirred by soul and prompted a deeper response. We talked about the value of sitting alone, focusing singularly on an individual that matters to you and then trying to carve out a message that will be meaningful to them. I told my former student that frequently when I send a sincere message of hope and encouragement, I hear back from the receiver saying something like, "I can't tell you how much your card meant to me. I needed to hear that." Furthermore, I told her that in the giving of a heartfelt message, as the writer I get so much value from the act of writing, even when I don't get anything back. I know the book you hold is not perfect, but it is the result of years of trying to carve out a timely and meaningful message to those that work in or care about the profession I love, teaching.

From Jennifer Bowling, Instructional Leader, Stevens Point Area Senior High

Sometimes in life we come across people who make our lives better, that change our outlook and make us a better teacher and person. One day, by chance, Dr. Brad Kahrs and a few of his University of Wisconsin – Stevens Point practicum students came into my Advanced Algebra 2 class to observe my teaching. Our first conversation was about both teaching and our love of travel. On that day I had no idea that over the next few years I would have regular conversations with Brad that would push me to be a better teacher. We developed an ongoing conversation about education, endurance, professional development, mentoring, belief in our profession, and hope.

Brad has an uncanny ability to build relationships, to ask the right questions, and to have compassion through difficult conversations. His experiences in all aspects of education, as a teacher, an instructional coach and an instructor of future teachers in higher education, gives him the ability to relate to all people who are looking for inspiration, endurance, and passion in their career and their overall outlook.

As Brad states, "In the teaching profession there are too many 'broken' teachers, just going through the motions, unable to find that 'sweet spot' of teaching that allows them to consistently find the 'pace' that makes their work meaningful, purposeful, and joyful." Throughout the following pages, you will be inspired and shown how to find that "sweet spot" that brings you back to why you wanted to teach.

Throughout this book, Brad does a phenomenal job of weaving his two passions together, teaching and running. His stories of endurance through 100-mile races and his career in education develop a connection that both motivates and gives the reader hope and belief in the teaching profession. "Even when you feel like you can't take another step, you can find it within yourself to keep going… and even when you feel worse than you ever have before there will be miles ahead of you where you can find desire and energy and joy." Throughout these pages, Brad helps you to find that desire, energy, and joy.

When you start this book you will find it is hard to put down. Brad does an amazing job of making you want more, to not set it down. Reading this book is like the many conversations I have had with him. The time we had during the lunch meetings that we often share passes so quickly and leaves me wanting more. This book works to reignite your passion, your joy, your connections, and your endurance. My hope for you is that you will feel empowered to become the best teacher you can possibly be. That is what Brad has done for me throughout the years and conversations we have shared.

To the reader…

I am a Rocky fan (that will become evident in the pages ahead). The series of films starring Sylvester Stallone has provided me a source of inspiration since I first watched the original Rocky movie as a senior in high school back in 1976. This low-budget film captured the "rags to riches" story of an uneducated club fighter who gets an unlikely opportunity to fight for the heavyweight championship of the world. In the fifth installment of the series there is a moment when Rocky is knocked down and hurting, laying in the street after a series of blows from a boxer [Tommy Gunn] whom Rocky befriended and coached but then rejects and turns his back on Rocky. As Rocky lays beaten and barely conscious, he hears the voice of his former manager [Mick – played by Burgess Meredith (1907 – 1997)]. Mick's "ghost" says to Rocky, "Get up you son-of-a-bitch, Mickey loves you."

If you're reading this, it's because I was able to "get up" and finish the "fight." There was only one reason that I was able to find the endurance to keep going: LOVE. I have watched the teaching profession take a lot of "hits" over the past few years and this book is my offering of ideas & inspiration intended to help educators that are down and hurting stay in the fight. And it truly is a fight, a battle for the hearts and minds of our youth. The teaching profession entered the COVID-19 pandemic in 2020 already "staggered" and facing big challenges. The pandemic was traumatic, and we face an aftermath that is threatening the lifeblood of schools: the hearts of teachers.

Laura van Dernoot Lipsky, founder and director of the Trauma Stewardship Institute experienced what she described as a near-psychotic break which she attributed to years of witnessing and having intimate involvement in traumatic situations without the insight of how to sustain herself in such conditions. All teachers have experienced a degree of trauma. I know I have. Certainly, COVID has been the most traumatic event the teaching profession has ever encountered, and the teaching profession needs a special kind of support that helps teachers regroup and do more than bear the hard things that have come in the aftermath.

Early in my coaching career I attended a clinic where expert coaches shared their know-how of coaching endurance runners. One session I attended was given by an experienced and successful coach who shared the story of his top athlete winning the individual title in the most recent state championship event. He spoke about the science of running and shared his inner thoughts as he had watched the last half-mile of the 5,000-meter race. His words included specifics on the workouts of the champion athlete. He described how the workouts were specifically devised for the moment when his athlete surged to the lead and pulled away to victory. I distinctly remember his statement that it was solely the science of the workouts that resulted in victory. I also remember that even at a young age with minimal experience I held a deep certainty that big moments in running require much more than just an application of science.

I have spent most of my career as a teacher and coach searching for and trying to capture the "other stuff" that contributes to meaningful moments and lessons. This journey has often proved challenging and filled with rejection.

Yet the rewards have been priceless. As I've written and presented about the ideas and insights on the pages ahead, I often find myself feeling like this book is similar to the "memo" in the movie *Jerry Maguire*. The main character (Jerry, played by Tom Cruise), an agent for high profile athletes writes a message from the heart about what really matters in his profession. He shares this message with everyone in the large firm where he works and is rejected and ridiculed, even let go from the company he helped start. Fortunately, he stays the course and eventually learns what love really means and how to support another human being in becoming the best version of themselves. The tears and hugs shared with the only two who stayed by his side and believed in him (his wife and the lone athlete that retained Jerry's services) always touches my heart. Like Jerry I have felt the sting of rejection and ridicule. Like Jerry I have often wondered if I should be openly sharing the matters deep within my heart. But, also like Jerry, I have experienced the treasured results of staying the course, enduring a hard thing and turning it into something akin to glory.

Mid-career I decided to leave my job of 18 years in Michigan and take a similar position in a small town in western Colorado. Mostly this decision was made because my love for the mountains coincided with my oldest daughter choosing to pursue her undergraduate studies at Colorado State University. While many questioned my decision, this choice shaped my life in many ways. I learned a lot through this huge life change. One lesson I learned immediately came from my initial adventures on mountain trails. I had climbed a couple of 14,000-foot peaks prior to my move but now as a resident I was afforded frequent opportunities. I got serious about climbing high and conquering some of Colorado's renowned mountains. I noticed that the parking lots at many trailheads would be full or even overflowing, yet when I made my way to the peak there would be few, if any, people there. Perhaps this is a metaphor for the teaching life. The thought of climbing a big, beautiful mountain is exciting but the demands of a steep climb in thin air can easily dampen commitment and turn you back. Similarly, the challenges faced by teachers can turn one back from the wholeheartedness necessary to impact young lives.

After 12 years in Colorado, I returned to the Midwest, mostly because family needs combined with a seemingly rare opportunity to shape Teacher Development practices in Math Education. I remember on the very first weekend in central Wisconsin having the thought, "what have I done?" In that moment, I realized that the mountains had become part of me. Hiking in the mountains characterized a perfect balance of adventure, challenge, and beauty that provided me with a consistent source of inspiration. That longing has stuck with me, eventually bringing me back west to a home near the Wasatch mountains (and my three beautiful granddaughters). My son recognized this longing within me gave me a small gift, now stuck on the front of my refrigerator, with the following quote from John Muir: "The mountains are calling, and I must go."

If you have made it this far in the book, I thank you and offer the following two stories, crucial in the development of my perspective towards classroom teaching and eventually, Teacher Development.

1 – The beginnings of passion. As a youth all I wanted to do was play baseball. I grew up in a "hotbed" of baseball. Just down the street from my house was a park with multiple baseball fields. During the warmer months in my west Michigan hometown, I would spend much of my free time on these fields. It was assumed that a game was always waiting, and the rules and choice of field were determined by how many (nearly all my friends were baseball players) showed up. We even had spots near the baseball fields for one-on-one baseball games. I remember thinking that my older brother was weird because he typically slept in on Saturday mornings and then watched cartoons until noon. Why would you do that when you could be playing baseball? I loved the game, everything about it and I was surrounded by others who shared this love. BUT when I was 10 years old my parents decided to move out to the country, and I was ripped away from my friends and my own personal field of dreams. I was placed on a remote farm far away from what I knew and loved. I lost easy access of playing the game I loved and the strong support system that helped me develop skill and passion for the game. I felt like a caged animal wanting to be returned to the habitat in which I thrived. Back in the late 60's and early 70's competitive opportunities were hard to find beyond the short summer season found in some small community programs. I ended up inventing my own games. I pitched balls into the side of our farmhouse, trying to hit specific spots over and over. I hit rocks with a plastic bat from our gravel driveway over a faraway fence. Occasionally I would convince my brothers to play a baseball-related game or participate in some kind of drill (my favorite was called "Pepper" which was intended to develop bat-control and quickness). Mostly, I was on my own, left longing to play the game I loved. [Note: My baseball glove was my most prized possession. At night if I heard rain or thunder, I would panic if my glove was not near me and I would charge out into the night to make sure I didn't leave it outside.]

Eventually my dad noticed this longing. He embedded a pitching rubber in our gravel driveway and on many evenings, I would pitch to him. I can remember waiting for him on the steps of our farmhouse, holding my glove, his glove, and a baseball. There were times he wouldn't eat dinner or change out of his suit and tie before he would be crouching in a catcher's stance and coaching my development as a baseball (and later softball) pitcher. There is no doubt that a large share of my teaching & coaching perspective was shaped on a driveway, in a remote corner of Michigan, with a baseball in my hand. You see, my dad didn't just catch my throws, he coached me in "becoming a pitcher, not just a thrower." I think more than the lessons of pitch location, types of pitches (I distinctly remember learning how to throw a changeup), and situational pitching, I developed a thoughtful approach to the game. I became reflective and this informed my perspective and future development as a teacher and coach. I began to see how skill, know-how, and passion combined to make me successful on the mound and as a teammate. I learned that when you go the extra mile, there will be lonely stretches, but you will find more meaning and often more success.

Eventually circumstances and opportunities, among other things, led me to endurance running. But a seed was planted in those early days of learning how to be a pitcher.

2 – Another experience instrumental in shaping my perspective on teaching, learning, and teacher development occurred near the end of my undergraduate studies. During my student teaching placement, I found myself on my own trying to figure out how to survive. I was placed at an inner-city school in Grand Rapids, Michigan. That alone was challenging for someone that had lived a mostly sheltered and isolated life to that point. Still, what made it particularly difficult was being left on my own. My assigned mentor (and this is not an exaggeration) spent about 10 minutes in the classroom with me, choosing coffee and cigarettes in the teachers' lounge over support and instruction of a novice teacher (yes, this was before NO SMOKING lounges were a thing). Additionally, the supervisor from my college visited only twice. One of those visits was during a test which meant no conversation, no guidance, no help. I had never felt so alone and inadequate. Trial and error became my sole learning strategy. Long before the internet and the concept of learning communities I was left to "sink or swim." I mostly sank. Not only did this capstone experience come up short of having me prepared to lead a classroom but I also realized, repeatedly, that my math degree did little to help me teach math concepts to young learners (many who seemed to lack the aptitude and/or attitude necessary to engage with mathematics). Nevertheless, I learned, slowly, steadily and at times painfully. I created my own growth & development practices. I became familiar with a sense of struggle and failure. I learned where to search, how to listen, keen noticing skills but mostly an awareness that there must be a better way to become a teacher. The seeds that got planted years earlier, on a gravel driveway, gained some sturdy roots. I craved for someone to notice and take me under their wing, like my dad had done in helping me become a pitcher, not just a thrower. Looking back, this experience (or lack of experience) steeled me for the hard work of teaching and like a mountain climber I became more comfortable on the edge of a cliff. It was years later before I fully realized the value of owning my personal and professional growth & development. My extreme struggles and consistent failures allowed me to see the classroom like the back side of the farmhouse. As a beginning pitcher I tried to hit the right spot on that old farmhouse over and over. As a beginning teacher I tried to create the "right" lesson. At first it happened rarely but eventually I found the ability to "nail it" and create memorable experiences for my students more often. It still feels good thinking back to those moments when I got it right (after so many wrongs).

In the summer of 2022, I sat in a coffee shop in Wyoming, talking with a veteran teacher and coach. He spoke about the heartache and disappointment in feeling like he has never quite got it right. This teacher is broken-hearted with a sense of failure that seems to grow larger with each passing year. He shared that on the heels of COVID he feels more drained and defeated than ever and unable to generate the energy and enthusiasm his students deserve.

Our profession does not have good solutions for this situation, but help can be found. I know, I have been there. The teacher mentioned above is in the middle of his career. He has helped many students have high-quality experiences in the classroom and on the playing field, but he faces many more years in the classroom feeling that he has not accomplished much. He is struggling to find the sense of exhilaration that comes with knowing you are making a difference.

The middle miles of an ultramarathon can be tough miles. The adrenaline of the start is gone, and the elation of the finish line is far off. To run a successful race one must remain steady, focused on the task at hand, constantly monitoring one's condition in order to replenish one's body and mind with the right stuff. One must keep alive the vision of a grand finish. For the teacher mentioned above, the middle miles of his "race" have placed the question "Is it worth it?" in his head and heart. This has brought him to the brink. Having been on the brink of physical collapse and an emotional "giving in", I know this pain. However, I also know the rewards when you make it back from the brink.

Near the end of the K-12 chapter of my teaching career I was working in a middle school building. I taught 7th and 8th grade mathematics in the morning and had prep time and release time to provide teacher support in the afternoon. It was a schedule and role that fit me well. One August day just before students returned for classes, I witnessed the heart-wrenching demise of community and confidence. The lead administrator decided to "motivate" teachers by having individual conversations with each teacher and the administrative staff comprised of himself and two assistants. These conversations provided each teacher with their "cut score" (the number of students that had moved up a level of achievement minus the number of students that had dropped a level). Perhaps this plan had good intentions but what I observed that day brought me to the brink. One by one I watched a teacher enter a room where they would sit across the table from the three administrators and receive their cut score typically along with a message of "you need to do better." Some teachers were off the hook because their subject matter was not included in the state tests, therefore they had no cut scores and thus no mandate to improve. Most of the beginning teachers, several that I worked with on a weekly basis, entered the room in fear and left the room discouraged. These teachers, who would be meeting their new students the very next day, began the school year defeated. Even though my "cut scores" measured up (I was considered PROFICIENT), this was one of the most discouraging days of my career as a K-12 educator. Later that day, I was sitting at my computer writing a letter of resignation (I just couldn't live with the human devastation and loss of heart I had witnessed) when a colleague entered my room and helped bring me back from the brink. The conversation with a caring colleague rescued me in many ways. Having someone notice my deep discouragement and reach out with a powerful reminder of what really matters (and it surely isn't one administrator's use of achievement data to inappropriately measure teacher proficiency [rant over]) helped instigate a journey. One meaningful conversation, at just the right time, fortified me for the coming school year and mold a mission to create the vision and vocabulary to address the challenges teachers face that push them to the brink.

The above-mentioned journey has included the completion of a Doctorate Degree in Education with an emphasis in Teacher Leadership, a dozen years in Higher Education and many opportunities to sit with teachers and hear their stories. I have discovered a strong sense of reward in acknowledging the extreme challenge of "on the brink" moments in teachers' careers and shining light on them in a way that produces a solid perspective and lifeline of hope. Like a first-year teacher said to me in spring of 2021, "Thanks for changing my perspective on teaching. I used to think teaching was nothing more than helping students put right answers on worksheets. It is so much more." Sometimes all we need is a little perspective.

Helping teachers hold onto the "so much more" perspective is likely the strongest support that can be provided in these challenging times. I hope that the pages ahead enhance your ability to consistently see the "so much more" in the teaching life and share that message and accompanying actions with your students and colleagues.

The Disney movie Miracle captures a moment just before the game between the U.S. and the Soviet Union in the 1980 Olympics. The name of the movie represents the result. It truly was a miracle for a group of young hockey players, most having never played internationally, to defeat the heavily favored Russian team (who had crushed the U.S. team just a few days before the Olympics began). My favorite scene is the pre-game speech given by Coach Herb Brooks (played by Kurt Russell). The coach begins his message with "Great moments are born from great opportunities and that's what you have tonight. That's what you've earned tonight!" He closes the speech with "you were born to be hockey players. You were meant to be here. THIS IS YOUR TIME!" Even now just thinking about that group of young athletes playing with such energy, determination and BELIEF inspires me. As the game is about to end, with 3 seconds to go, Al Michaels says the famous line, "Do you believe in miracles?"

Tough times and hardships lie ahead for the teaching profession. Trying times that include many teachers leaving the profession, rampant discouragement, and a strong sense of disappointment are pointing us towards much-needed change. I believe that those teachers that stay and strive to maintain a wholeheartedness have boundless opportunities to shape the future of the teaching profession, helping children and adults alike have extraordinary experiences and a lifetime of living with so much more. This is YOUR time!

As mentioned earlier, I decided to pursue a Doctorate Degree after 25 years in K-12 education. Thinking this terminal degree would provide significant opportunities for me to impact the teaching profession, I worked hard. I read and wrote voraciously. I studied often in the pre-dawn hours while holding onto my job as a classroom teacher. The final stages of the degree requirements included the completion of a dissertation. Research from this challenging project is sprinkled throughout the pages ahead. I began work on the dissertation with the intention of uncovering and disclosing mentoring practices that most effectively help beginning teachers. Pieces of that worthy goal were uncovered. However, the real story of this two-year research project was discovering the barriers in providing meaningful and lasting professional growth & development for teachers. Overcoming these barriers is no easy task because the key to generating endurance lies in the heart. For teachers that strive to impact lives, it is the heart that eventually will drive behavior, fulfillment, and development. Sadly, I also discovered that matters of the heart are rarely acknowledged and addressed in a consistent and meaningful way. Accessing and attending to the hearts of teachers needs to play a robust role in professional development plans.

I have realized there exists many connections between endurance in running and endurance in teaching. Throughout the more than 55 years that I have been in a classroom and actively participated in running events I continually stumble upon lessons within one endeavor that powerfully informs the other. One strong similarity between running and teaching was how I began. Starting from ground zero as a runner and beginning a teaching career ill-prepared led to painful lessons in both of my chosen pursuits. Perhaps experiences like jumping over rattlesnakes, running away from Momma Bears (yeah, I know you're not supposed to run from bears) and biting dogs, getting lost in the wilderness without food and water, trying to stay ahead of biting flies and hearing the words CAN'T and SHOULDN'T helped prepare me for a career in teaching where painful or scary encounters and constant uncertainty are different but just as difficult to keep going afterward.

In the pages ahead I will share many insights and stories of how my life as an endurance runner and educator coincided to provide a strong sense of purpose and meaning. Andy Andrews, in his book *The Noticer*, says the following, "Many of life's treasures remain hidden from us simply because we never search for them." It is my hope and intention to share the treasures I've found because I have been willing to risk, able to bear the inevitable heartache, and continually embrace opportunities to share the journey with others in the greatest of professions. I offer a summary of the five main sections within the text as a preview to what's ahead for you, the reader.

PART 1 — INTRODUCTION

The "researchy" part of this book brings together real data, several decades of lived experience as a teacher and coach, real stories from inside and outside the classroom, and an extensive number of good ideas synthesized while writing and presenting at state and national conferences. It is my hope that the stories (presented in italics) give the ideas of endurance clarity and life. Many of the references in this chapter are from leaders in the field and were collected over a decade or more spent searching for the secrets of Teacher Development.

PART 2 — MOVING THROUGH THE AFTERMATH OF COVID

This chapter recognizes that many teachers have become disheartened and restive and are no longer willing to be highly compliant and lowly paid professionals. During the intense COVID years of 2020-2021 many teachers expressed a sense of being "lost" and shared the thought "This is NOT teaching!" The very thing that gave me the greatest sense of reward, those teachers in my circle, now poured discouragement my way. I grieved for them, often. Teachers need to be highly valued and appropriately supported. Here I share the results of many hours spent uncovering and summarizing the thoughts and experiences from 25 excellent educators as they pondered their futures and the future of the teaching profession beyond the pain and struggles of COVID.

PART 3 — COMPONENTS OF ENDURANCE

This section provides a perspective of resilience and how teachers need a special brand of resilience that I choose to call endurance. Endurance is more than resilience because of the important distinction between the two concepts. The distinction is that endurance turns tough times and painful moments into glory. Within the components of endurance, I provide a "snapshot" description of each of these matters of the heart that can be nurtured and grown which then lays a foundation of endurance.

PART 4 — CREATING A CULTURE OF ENDURANCE

I once had a colleague, who later become the lead administrator in the building where I worked, tell me that I have been "spoiled" relative to my perspective on issues of teamwork and culture. The reason for this "spoiled-ness" was that I have experienced the best of team and community. This makes working with less than the best frequently disappointing. There is no doubt that with a strong dose of TOGETHER in the workplace everyone does work and life better. It is my intention, rather than provide a list of best practices, to share 10 principles of team and culture that I have been fortunate enough to experience throughout my life. I hope these principles will aid in facilitating a vision of the kind of community that can be built in every school, one that enhances endurance.

PART 5 — WHERE DO WE GO FROM HERE?

In a profession that currently works so hard to do things right this chapter includes a presentation of "right" things teachers can do to infuse that little bit of glory that lies within each of us into their own lives and the profession as a whole.

PART 6 — THE FINISH LINE.

The final chapter is a collection of tributes to several enduring educators that have been a precious part of my life. I "tie a bow" on the book with several personal descriptions of inspiring people and uplifting actions.

Before letting you forge ahead into the collection of ideas, insights, and stories on the coming pages I wanted to share a portion of a journal entry I wrote in a personal journal sometime in the last year. I wrote the following in 2021: *"Writing messages to others that encourage and inspire has been a lifelong practice, something that calls to my heart and brings me to life."*

Just as there are barriers to Professional Growth & Development for teachers, there are also barriers in the becoming a writer. I feel those barriers nearly every single day. Paulo Coelho, author of *The Alchemist*, indicated that there are four obstacles for potential authors to overcome in achieving their dream of a completed creative work. Three of those obstacles constantly cloud my head and heart. Coelho's first obstacle is the world telling us that our dream is impossible. For me this comes in a voice saying "Can't" or "It doesn't matter." The second obstacle that I continually struggle with is that in trying to live the creative life one must often abandon those they love. This is the sacrifice I have made, and I thank my family and closest friends for helping me feel loved even when I am undeserving. The third obstacle has become part of my life for a long time. Writers and likely all those who try to create something meaningful will face the fear of rejection. I have suffered greatly in overcoming this obstacle. I hope in (finally) finishing this collection of my best ideas for helping teachers endure the intense challenges they face I will provide just enough encouragement and inspiration to keep you going in a way that provides constant affirmation that you were born to be a teacher.

Early in my career I was told by my school district's Superintendent, "Brad, you have to stop caring so much." I never did; stop caring that is. I hope that care is evident and uplifting to you as you read. As a coach and endurance athlete I was fortunate to have witnessed some incredible performances of endurance and gain insight into these performances. I am certain you have heard a version of the following: they put such heart into what they do. Endurance racing requires great heart and when you see someone race with heart the performance sticks with you. It is more than the result – so much more. I can still remember the first time I witnessed this kind of performance when as a 13-year-old I watched Steve Prefontaine race the 5,000-meters in the 1972 Olympics. The memory of that race brings me back to the young boy who was just beginning his journey of endurance running and racing, sitting in front of the television and feeling the struggle, the disappointment of missing a medal, but most of all the heart he put into the effort. Years later, I was able to be included with a small group of people invited to preview the Warner Bros. production *Without Limits*, the story of Steve Prefontaine. I got to sit with actors and actresses, champions of the sport, and some of Pre's family to view the yet to be named and uncompleted movie. It was an amazing privilege, one that I will never forget. To be in a room with a group of people that shared a belief that "Pre" lived and race with heart in a special way impacted my life in many ways.

Later in my coaching career I attempted to capture in words what it means to race with heart. I turned that effort into an essay that I shared with a summer camp which included teams from four different schools. In the essay I acknowledged that you can't race with heart every time. But you can race with heart when it counts. Similarly, you can't teach with great heart every single day BUT you can when it counts. It takes extraordinary effort, time, sacrifice and energy to teach with heart but IT IS WORTH IT! On the pages ahead I make many connections between teaching and endurance running. Some will resonate with you. I hope the one that sticks is that both endeavors, when done well take great heart and when we race with heart or teach with heart, we CAN create unforgettable moments. I wish you the best in finding and replenishing your unforgettableness.

In chapter 2 I provide some information and stories from over two dozen teacher interviews that I completed early in the summer of 2022. I had asked each of the participating teachers three questions that I thought might provide fuel for the homestretch of my work on this project and inform the teaching profession as the trauma of COVID is left behind. I completed one interview with a teacher in mid-career that admitted his job has never been harder. As we discussed challenges in developing endurance, he turned the tables on me and asked, "So what's your secret? You were a teacher for 40 years. How did you do it? How did you endure?" My initial response to him serves as an encouragement to you – READ ON!

TEACHING WITH ENDURANCE

Endurance is not just the ability to bear a hard thing, but to turn it into glory.

INTRODUCTION

The runner had covered over 80 miles of a 100-mile race through the hills of Vermont. It was a long, grueling day on the trail. Night was approaching; the miles ahead would require him to focus at a higher level. Rocks and tree roots always seemed larger in the dark and getting up after a fall is tougher late in a race. Yet, he had prepared, in these days before headlamps, a high-quality flashlight with spare batteries was in his pack, and the trail was lit with glow sticks, illuminating the trail. While his pace slowed a bit he continued steadily towards the finish line when suddenly the glow sticks disappeared (it was discovered later that a group of partying teenagers had removed them, hanging them on their car's rearview mirror). Relying on the flashlight and yellow pie plates attached to trees that marked the way for those following the trail in daylight the runner continued through the dark forest confidently until the flashlight went out. Thinking that it needed new batteries the runner replaced them and found the flashlight would still not work. With no other option the runner began shuffling forward hoping that the next aid station would appear quickly. Any attempt to run resulted in hitting trees; his pace became a slow walk, hands in front of his face to fend off branches. He had prepared for these dark miles. Why was he forced to tread wearily and painfully, now bloodied from too many encounters with trees? His race, now a survival test, diminished to a goal of just making it to the next aid station where a new light awaited.

Much of my life I have strived to build endurance. I have embraced the life and habits of an endurance runner. As I enter the last "laps" of my professional "race" it seems that endurance is needed in the teaching profession more than ever. Teachers, as a whole, are struggling, wandering through a "dark night" with expectations often unmet, meaning unfound, and continuity absent. Doubt and discouragement abound, intensified with a constant mantra of accountability and a hyperfocus on achievement data. Teacher support is typically couched with a message of "or else" or another requirement added to an already hectic day.

My dissertation, completed in 2011, uncovered strong evidence of this loss of endurance. Teacher attrition is a growing challenge in schools across the U.S. that sees approximately 50% of teachers leaving the profession within 5 – 6 years. Attrition has created a cycle of inexperience that leaves schools struggling to have quality teachers lead classrooms. Endurance is required of those that stay in the profession, yet it appears that upwards of 80% remain in a "survival state."

Many runners have an expression for those moments when all energy, drive, and desire are gone and the ability to run strongly fades leaving one to stumble along, slowly, in a "survival shuffle." Once in survival shuffle mode it becomes incredibly difficult to raise one's head, lift the knees, and continue towards the finish line with confidence and determination. In long endurance races help is typically a well-timed aid station where a runner can re-fuel and receive encouragement or comes in the form of a pacer, someone who will run alongside and with their presence remove a portion of the uncertainty and difficulty in setting the pace and staying on course.

Too many teachers leave the profession just about the time they become efficient and effective. Others stay but just survive or coast, unable or unwilling to do the things that make a lasting impact on the minds and lives of children. Yet, there seems to be about 10% of teachers who become teachers of *impact*. The term *impact* includes noticing and embracing the opportunities to make a lasting difference in the lives and successes of children and finding the ways and means to inspire children to succeed. The current standards movement and the accompanying narrow measures of teaching success results in a high level of discouragement for many teachers which "takes a heavy toll on motivation, loyalty, and performance" (Bolman & Deal, 2001, p. 6). What is it about some teachers that provides them with the endurance to not only bear the difficulty of teaching in the current age but to turn it into something glorious?

This book intends to illuminate aspects of endurance that seem to provide teachers of impact with the ability to avoid a "survival state" and continue moving forward in the long, arduous task of teaching at a time of great discouragement and uncertainty. The teaching profession needs rescuing but that rescue mission needs to come from within the profession: teachers themselves. Along with a clarification and description of endurance factors for educators, stories of real experiences will help clarify critical issues in the personal and professional growth of teachers.

I share here one of the most enduring lessons of my more than 39 years as an educator. It was a lesson that came at one of the lowest moments of my early professional life. Now more than 20 years later I have gained clarity on how valuable this lesson proved to me (and the novice educators I have worked with since).

November 1999! I coached a group of young men that included my son. This group had developed into a highly regarded cross country team. Early in the season a coach's poll rated the team #1 in the state of Michigan and that top rating remained throughout the remainder of the season. Despite some late season setbacks in the form of illness, injury, and ineligibility the team set a school record point total at the Regional Championship, qualifying for the state finals as the favorite. With a "jaw-dropping" performance one week before the State Championship the team seemed poised to win it all. In a personal journal I recorded the following: "I have known these seniors for most of their lives. I have shared so much with them…when they lined up together for the last time, so ready to lay claim to the pinnacle of their sport, they slipped…they lost their grasp of team, of desire, of commitment, of destiny." In the race that meant the most they came up short, finishing a disappointing third.

The lesson began one week later at the State of Michigan Coaches Clinic. Still stinging from a painful loss, I stood with a colleague minutes before the keynote address when a rival coach approached and said, "Man, did you screw up last week. What did you do wrong with your team's workouts?" These words echoed in my mind throughout the following year. I had always approached my role of coach with a high degree of reflection, research, and attempt to bring together components of science, knowledge, emotion, and inspiration. My workouts (I felt) were well-planned with a balance of challenge, variety, and sensible expectations. In the arena where I felt most competent, I was now filled with doubt.

*The following season with a group of young boys that had watched their teammates the previous season fail their biggest "test" a State Championship was won. A team unranked at the beginning of the season, improved at an incredible rate and captured victory in the same venue they had watched the painful defeat of their older teammates just one year earlier. This unexpected victory resulted in numerous coaches, at the very same coaches clinic, seeking the "secret" of my workouts that had produced a State Title seemingly out of nowhere. I was asked repeatedly for the workouts I had implemented during the final weeks of the season that had produced a peak performance. It was then I learned a lesson that has stuck with me, a lesson of endurance – **It's not about the workouts**! Achievement, in the long run, is about so much more and begins with matters of the heart.*

It seems that the teaching profession has become like the coaches described in the paragraph above, wanting "quick-fix" solutions. With the clarity gained from the exhilarating victory balanced with the heartache of disappointing loss, I realized that when working with young people, even when the science of their workouts is well-planned and effectively implemented, there will still be challenges and setbacks. It is NOT about the workouts! Similarly, in the teaching profession, there is so much more to providing enduring lessons than just content and process which manifests as an over-emphasis on programs and curriculum and a hyper-focus on standards and measurements in the meeting of these standards. As the graphic below reveals, teaching with endurance lies at the intersection of three realms: intellect & knowledge, process & method, and the human component of inspiration. The book you hold is what I've lived and learned regarding the pursuit of helping both athletes and teachers develop the ability to turn the challenges of running or teaching into something glorious and significant.

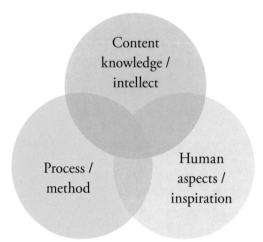

Parker Palmer, in his book *The Courage to Teach,* acknowledged that each educator "has a sacred duty to teach particular knowledge and skills" and yet each teacher also needs to serve as a catalyst to "lead out" those gifts and qualities that are within each student. This work is a teacher's most important task and requires tapping the world of inspiration in unique and powerful ways in order to unleash the best each student has to give. Hargreaves (2003), in a large-scale research project concerned with school improvement and reform, voiced concern that a "hyperfocus" on the priorities of performance standards could "actively undermine the emotional dimensions of educating" and ultimately leave no space for "all those things that fuel the passion to teach" (p. 60). The result of a standards mind-set, in addition to the humbling and difficult work of teaching, creates a hopelessness that is difficult to overcome. There is strong evidence that potential results of the standards movement are a narrower curriculum and teachers who are discouraged with the loss of trust and autonomy and have become less innovative with their instruction.

A few years ago, my oldest daughter asked me to serve as pacer in her first marathon. As a lifelong runner myself it was particularly rewarding to be able to participate in a marathon where my two oldest children were running their first, and to be asked to run by the side of my daughter in an event that was a huge physical challenge. Early in the race, after about 10 miles of steady, consistent running, I had to use the porta-john at one of the aid stations. I told my daughter to keep running and that I would catch up soon. After taking care of my business, I grabbed the door handle to exit the porta-john and whether intentionally or unintentionally, someone had left "crap" all over the handle. For a few seconds I allowed the discomposure of "crap" on my hand, in the middle of a race, to steal my focus of what really mattered. Fortunately, I was able to quickly realize that I needed to get back in the race if I was going to catch up to my daughter now minutes ahead. I splashed water from the aid station on my hand, cleaning up as best I could, and put the discomfort aside. I will never forget how I felt during the final miles of the marathon, side-by-side with my daughter, passing dozens of runners who had given into the pain and fatigue, and sharing that special sense of accomplishment as the finish line came into view. The embrace we shared at the finish line remains with me still…it endures. Yet, it might have been lost if I had allowed the "crap" to steal the moment.

Beginning teachers need help in "seeing beyond the crap." The first two years of teaching are typically demanding and disheartening, yet the experiences during this time largely determine the commitment and attitude of new teachers. Although some assistance exists for beginning teachers, the literature indicates that the quality of this support is inconsistent, often failing to help teachers succeed in the classroom and stay in the profession for the long haul. The National Commission on Teaching and America's Future [NCTAF] affirmed findings that the most professional development activities for teachers are district-sponsored professional development events that are often generic in nature. Common professional growth activities include work on curriculum committees, professional association-sponsored events, summer college courses, and national board certification requirements. However, in many cases, these professional development practices prove inconsistent, shallow, ineffective and produce little or no change in the classroom habits and practices of teachers. NCTAF indicated a need for a reinvention of teacher preparation and professional development because even well-educated, well-prepared teachers encounter challenges that appear insurmountable and situations that are unstable.

The first few years of teaching are a critical time for most educators. Early in a teacher's career comes a choice to leave, stay in a "survival state," or move to an "impact stage." The term *survival* (mentioned earlier) implies getting through each day. However, the term *impact* (also mentioned earlier) includes noticing and embracing the opportunities to make a difference in the lives and learning of children and finding the ways and means to inspire children to achieve. With nearly half of teachers leaving the profession within their first six years and many others becoming discouraged in their work few teachers reach the impact stage. Barth (2001) indicated that this discouragement can result in a loss of a teacher's becoming a difference-maker. Palmer (2003) said this loss makes change and reform inaccessible.

Teachers need support in ways that extend beyond presentations about innovative processes, lessons, strategies, or recent test results. Sergiovanni (2005) indicated a critical priority for schools with the following:

> Once human resources are built up in both skill and heart, then the school is better able to acquire and develop new and better ways to function, to create opportunities, and to exploit circumstances in a manner that results in more effective school performance. Because of the unpredictability of the world and the limits of human rationality, it makes sense to emphasize building capabilities of people. (p. 39)

Additional examination of how professional development can bring together matters of intellect and inspiration is necessary. Sergiovanni (2005) stated that these matters fall separately into the "*lifeworld*" and "*systemsworld.*" While the "*systemsworld*" includes management strategies the "*lifeworld*" includes issues of human capital. I intend to shed light on how the connection of these two worlds can occur in schools and the professional development experiences of beginning teachers. Hargreaves (2003) stated that professional development "rarely reaches people's souls". With fervent consideration of how to effectively support and develop beginning teachers, the opportunity to transform society lies within the grasp of educators who mentor, lead, or work with new teachers. Building the capacity of beginning teachers makes a positive difference in communities and school cultures. When teachers are committed to their school and the teaching profession, children benefit (Sergiovanni, 2005). Society is stronger when children receive guidance from educators who seek a life of making a difference for children. Fostering and enhancing a mission mindset of making a positive difference in the lives of children within the teaching profession should be at the forefront of professional development.

Years ago, I coached a talented young runner who had qualified for the State Finals in cross country all 4 years of her high school career. Most would consider this a successful career. However, on the evening before her 4th State Finals race, she approached me in tears. With her last race before her, "Kate" expressed deep sadness and regret with the following, "I have never hurt during a race. I have always stayed comfortable, unwilling or unable to hurt for my team or myself. Is there something wrong with me? How can I find the ability and desire to push myself past pretty good?" Despite being seen as highly successful this athlete experienced an inner emptiness because she was unable to unlock her very best, feeling she had settled for less. There is a certain pain in settling for pretty good.

Preparation to teach requires a wholeheartedness that easily slips away. When running a long race, it is critical to pace oneself, finding that "sweet spot" of effort that allows one to compete to the best of their ability. With the right pace a prepared runner can efficiently cover many miles. However, it is easy to get lured into running too hard early in the race, become depleted, and end up struggling to maintain the pace that leads to a successful race. If you stand near the finish line of a long race you will see many "broken" runners, heads down, happy just to be done with the race. Of course, you will also see some runners who finish strong, joy evident on their face, as they cross the finish line. In the teaching profession there are too many "broken" teachers, just going through the motions, unable to find that "sweet spot" of teaching that allows them to consistently find the "pace" that makes their work meaningful, purposeful, and joyful. It is also true that some finish a race strong because they have never pushed hard and like "Kate" they feel unfulfilled.

It seems that much of the preparation practices for teachers, both preservice and postemployment, focuses on the *systemsworld* (Sergiovanni, 2005). Schon (1983) called this the "high, hard ground" (p. 145) of standards and uniform practices based on theory and rationality. Rational solutions do not always solve the challenges of teaching. Schon called many of the challenges facing teachers the "swampy lowlands" of schools (p. 145). Success for teachers frequently requires a descent to these low and emotionally taxing places. It is a crucial challenge for beginning teachers to prepare for this aspect of the job. Hargreaves & Fullan, as early as 1992, affirmed this with their finding that teacher development typically stays trapped in the knowledge and skill development arena. Lefstein (2005) indicated that a focus on just the rational vision of education often blinds "us to the realities and possibilities revealed by the personal, experiential side" (p. 333).

Teachers enter the profession with much to learn. With such a large learning agenda beginning teachers often leave the profession or stay and cling to practices and attitudes that help them survive but do not provide fulfillment or best serve the needs of students. New teachers develop coping strategies to just survive and fail to develop endurance in the profession and reach the stage of reflective and self-challenging practices that result in successful teaching for a career.

When knowledge is measured by a student's ability to memorize facts without a connection to the lived world and separate from interpretation, learning becomes trivial. Similarly, by making teaching a technical process, a series of generic "just do this" strategies or hints and tips meant to help students score well, the teaching profession is diminished. When teaching is trivialized meaning vanishes, endurance fades, and the wholeheartedness possessed by many teachers is lost.

Currently, many schools follow a Professional Learning Community (PLC) model of professional interaction. In the fragmented and frenzied lives of k-12 teachers this model helps create a focus on some aspects of teaching (typically measures of achievement that align with state standards or district curriculum). With teaching becoming increasingly complex and, knowledge and expertise relative to teaching evolving rapidly this model can be extremely helpful for beginning teachers. However, despite the collaborative nature of this model with the potential to enhance curriculum and instruction there is a huge "hole" in this model that becomes evident in the commitment of teachers for the long haul. Too many teachers, burdened with additional duties of management and supervision, struggle to grow professionally.

In my previous research, intended to illuminate mentoring practices that most effectively helped beginning teachers, it was determined that while PLC gatherings served as a resource for instructional guidance, early service teachers did not feel safe sharing issues of struggle or discouragement. It seems that the process of PLC obscures community. A common response from beginning teachers relative to sharing struggles with their building or grade level PLC indicated strong unwillingness or inability to delve into issues of personal difficulty, discouragement, or disappointment.

In striving to improve schools, teachers have been burdened with many additional duties and demands beyond leading academic development. Often the most important things, the things that matter most, are not allowed to "take root." It is my contention that creating trusting and respectful relationships in schools and classrooms is the indispensable and most crucial element to learning and making schools places that students <u>want to be</u>. Despite the intent to create community in our schools, the level of controls, audits, and monitoring placed on teachers often removes the heart and soul of teaching. In the effort to improve student outcomes the teaching profession is not effectively availing itself of the very thing that might provide the most powerful assistance – community/team.

Earlier, I provided a description of my biggest professional disappointment which was followed by perhaps my biggest success and greatest lesson. On the day of the disappointment, I witnessed a huge loss. The loss occurred long before the final scores were determined. In Michigan, the state finals in cross country are run at Michigan Speedway in Brooklyn, Michigan. The starting line lies on the immense infield and is surrounded by a concrete track intended for car racing and bleachers for thousands of spectators. It can be an overwhelming atmosphere for young runners, unlike any previous experience. With approximately 300 of Michigan's finest distance runners lined up, all with the goal of running fast, the first few minutes of the race often determines success because many choose to fail. The confusion and fast pace can result in runners unable to compete well after leaving the stadium 800 meters into the 5,000-meter race. In 1999, our mantra was "out the gate together." I knew that being physically close to each other during the first few minutes of the race would provide the team with an inner peace and confidence that would translate into a strong team effort. I also understood that despite being a team of veterans this was a team that could easily make mistakes early in the race that would steal the strong effort they were capable of, mostly because each of them battled with a habit of putting themselves ahead of their team. I still remember the feeling of loss as I watched my team disintegrate in those first few minutes. In their desire to succeed individually they ran too hard and lost their connection to team. They were swallowed up in the pack early in the race. Some of them panicked and tried to run harder and others gave in and slowly drifted deeper into the "sea" of runners. The demise of WE occurred because of the "disease" of ME.

Building a culture of togetherness where learning is consistently modeled as a happy, enjoyable, enlivening, and fulfilling experience along with constantly reviving a desire to impact young lives just might be the most important factor in long-term success of schools. There are no "quick fixes" on the path to team building. It is difficult to cull data to show immediate impact of team building intents and culture creating efforts. Yet there is strong evidence that when authentic teams exist in schools change and growth are more easily accessed, student achievement rises, retention and commitment are strengthened, and fulfillment enhanced.

However, the current landscape of education sees teachers constantly being monitored, controlled, and audited. Teacher gatherings (meetings) typically focus solely on components of the systemsworld: schedules, curriculum, evaluation, mandates, and assessment. Becoming a teacher of impact is not a "one and done" deal, it is progressive and requires great effort. Just like in the realm of endurance racing, professional breakthroughs for teachers often come only after long periods of struggle, frustration, or remaining at a consistent but ordinary level. Distance running can become drudgery without performance breakthroughs. Similarly, teaching can become a very flat career without the intense meaningfulness and fulfillment that comes with the sense that you are impacting young lives.

As a coach of endurance runners, I was constantly searching for how to unlock each athlete's full potential. It was frustrating when runners would come up short of their goals and the reason for this "failure" was unclear. Often, one week after an excellent performance some runners would be unable to demonstrate a similar level of mental and physical toughness in their next race. I sensed that the answers to breakthrough performances lay at the intersection of three worlds: physical, intellectual, and spiritual/emotional/inspirational.

Early in my coaching career we found a special place for our summer camp. On the shores of Lake Michigan near Glen Arbor, Michigan we created our own running paradise. With rustic cabins and easy access to Lake Michigan's shoreline and beautiful trails, each day captured the imagination of the team's vision of running adventure. With spectacular views all around we found the ability to set down the outside world with all its distractions and intensely focus on "becoming." This becoming included the individual pursuits of each runner but also the team component so valuable in meaningful and lasting experiences.

Our camp included elements of fun, discipline, goal setting, and learning, but in looking back there was one component that made our camp more than just an athletic experience. We even had a name for it: Miller Hill. Miller Hill was a nearby place, high above two beautiful lakes. Really just a viewpoint for cars to drive in, park and provide a majestic view of the area, but during camp week it became so much more than a place; it was an event. Miller Hill was a crucial experience for the teams I coached. It became a special experience. We went to Miller Hill for our team talks and figuratively rise high by digging deep. Miller Hill was the spot where coaches and athletes were granted "permission" to be completely open and honest. On Miller Hill the burdens and failures of the past were discussed, the hopes and goals for the future were shared, and many tears were shed. Miller Hill was the where & how we determined and displayed what we stood for as a team and what we would strive for as individuals.

Miller Hill became our landmark of digging deep. "Digging deep" means giving all of oneself in a special way. It involves sharing the best of yourself and looking for the best in others. It means forging ahead on a path that is often difficult and uncertain because of a vision of excellence and significance. Finally, it includes the desire to break down the "little shields" which we all carry around with us in the battle of life that prevent deep connectedness. The significance of our time together was enhanced because of an intentionality to dig deep on Miller Hill.

THE COVID CHAPTER — MOVING THROUGH THE AFTERMATH

Late in the fall of 2021 in serving my role of student teacher supervisor I arrived early to an elementary school in Salt Lake City, Utah to observe a third-grade math lesson. I had worked with the student teacher previously in math education courses. She was an excellent student and a determined teacher with much potential. We had discussed the lesson plan prior to this teaching encounter and were both looking forward to the lesson enactment and post-lesson debrief. Just as the lesson was underway a building administrator walked into the classroom trailed by approximately 20 fourth-grade students. The student teacher (with no warning) was now required to teach a math lesson to a group of third-graders while monitoring and engaging with a group of older students she had never met. The reason for this inappropriate challenge was two-fold: a teacher in the building had recently quit and there were no available substitute teachers. Things went fine but lost was a significant opportunity for teacher development. Instead of a conversation fully focused on the student teacher's growth as an instructor of mathematics the debrief became entangled with frustration and discouragement. Instead of an opportunity to discuss a unique enactment of math pedagogy the student teacher had learned in her college studies the experience of being overwhelmed with management left the student drained and distracted.

In this post-COVID world (oh how I hope the challenge of COVID is ending) we need to reconsider aspects of how we do schooling. Prior to the pandemic the teaching profession was already struggling with issues of attrition, motivation, and commitment. The trauma of COVID hit teachers hard. There is no doubt that the accumulation of big and small losses, challenges and tensions around masks, quarantines, vaccinations, school closures, online teaching, increased or uncertain expectations, and more took a toll on teachers. We need a newness to the profession: some new expectations, some new habits, some new resources, some new rewards. We need to recreate the teaching profession in a way that makes sense and fits with our changed and more challenging post-COVID world.

On my 63rd birthday (May 15, 2022) CBS aired an episode of *60 Minutes* that included a report on the plight of teachers. Within this 18-minute segment it was said that teaching has "become an undesirable profession." It struck me again! We must do something to rescue the teaching profession. My contribution to this effort is in your hands. This book sprung from a research project intended to uncover effective ways to help beginning teachers through the practice of mentoring. That research project used teacher voices to frame teacher development and produce a vision of what mentoring might be. I was able to uncover significant obstacles in teacher development which created possibility for what the role of teacher educator and mentor can be. This shaped the next 12 years of my life. I saw intense need for novice teachers back then, but teachers of all experience levels <u>need so much more now</u>.

A recent news report out of Charlotte, North Carolina stated that the teaching profession needs "revamping." Part of the problem, according to the report, is that "teacher voices are not heard." In the *60 Minutes* episode mentioned earlier one of the teachers interviewed had taught for nearly 20 years at the secondary level but had left the profession because in her words "Teaching was taking too much from me." I believe the profession needs more than revamping. It needs a rescue and if it's going to be rescued most of the answers for what the rescue effort looks like need to come from teachers.

The dark, difficult days of COVID might be fading but the trauma has taken much from the hearts and lives of teachers. During tough times most teachers rally. They do what it takes for their students. They strive to overcome challenges. But now the storm has subsided and my fear mirrors Laura van Dernat Lipsky's [Trauma Stewardship Institute] warning, "it's the aftermath that will destroy us." The teaching profession was already teetering and COVID threatens to push us over the edge where desperation and despair are waiting. I fear the longing and rush for normalcy will shove teachers fully off the cliff.

As an endurance runner myself and later as a coach of endurance runners it has always amused me that within the pages of running magazines you consistently find articles that promise great race results with minimal training. In this hour of massive struggle to return schools to normal we must recognize that IT WILL NOT BE EASY! We must help teachers regroup! Hard times require more than will power and compliance to mandates and standards. We must help teachers replenish the things that help them be difference-makers in the lives of children. This crucial work takes a strength of mind, heart, and spirit.

In the summer of 1990, my cross-country team camp welcomed and hosted another team coached by an individual that was just beginning his coaching career. One morning I took both boys' teams for a run along the Lake Michigan shoreline with the intention of covering a few miles along the lake and then running over the dunes to a parking lot where my assistant coach would be waiting with a van to shuttle the boys back to camp. The runners covered the shoreline miles much faster than I had planned. As we headed over the dunes, I thought I would add an element of adventure. Since we had plenty of time and I thought I knew the dunes well I decided to head off course for a few extra miles. I ended up getting approximately 20 boys lost on the dunes for a few hours. Immediately upon realizing my dilemma I called all the boys together and asked them to stay put while I climbed to a high point and got my bearings. While I was away several athletes had scattered because they "knew" which way to go (they didn't). For more than 2 hours I chased down the lost teenagers and searched for the quickest way to rescue the runners, now dehydrated, in a state of panic and doubting the wisdom of their coach. Eventually I spotted a Park Ranger who called the camp, and a rescue team came in vans to take us a now much longer distance back to our camp's location. I was physically exhausted and emotionally spent from facing the fear of losing young runners in a sunbaked wilderness. I will never forget the frustration of discovering that some in our group abandoned the team and sought their own rescue. Years later I learned that the dunes are constantly shifting and the trail I knew so well was gone. The result was a near disaster.

As our country and the teaching profession regroups, I think we must be careful regarding any attempt to return to normal. We need a new normal. States and school districts across the country, in combatting extensive losses from attrition and lack of replacements from the traditional pipelines of new teachers, have adjusted certification requirements or removed them altogether. Certification does not guarantee preparation. There are strong indications that untrained or poorly trained individuals leave the profession at two to three times the rate of highly trained teachers. We need teachers who are prepared to not only deliver lessons of content but also model qualities like kindness, integrity, and empathy. We need teachers who strive to shape the future by shaping the children they work with every day.

As a coach of distance runners at the high school level I experienced heartache when some of athletes on the team quit after turning 16. Looking back, it seems that this was a crucial age for high school athletes. At this point in their young lives, they suddenly had many more options for the after-school hours and weekends. Many could now drive and chose to work more hours so they could buy their own car and experience more freedom. The discipline and hard physical training required in becoming a distance runner lost its attraction for some. I can remember hearing the words "I just want to have fun" from most of these former athletes. It hurt! As a coach I had poured a lot of time and care into someone who leaves the team. I know that the early years of a running career includes the tug away from the single-heartedness demanded of endurance athletes. Only with a strong vision of the meaningful benefits do teenagers choose and stick with the more challenging path. A consistent coaching practice of mine was to bring back alumni athletes to share an "it was worth it" message. I know I heard the words "I wish I would have…" from many of those athletes who left the team at 16 as they graduated and went out into the world.

I am fortunate to have experienced the best of a teaching life. As I look back at four decades of teaching and coaching it is the wonderful connections, I share with many students and educators that are my greatest rewards. As I strive to complete this writing project, I realize I am creating a souvenir of my journey in education and the lessons I've collected along the way. Still, I want to draw on some of those wonderful connections I share within the profession that will not only propel me forward towards the finish line but also shed some light on the state of our profession. I believe that the condition of the hearts of caring and committed teachers is far more important than statistics on attrition and achievement.

In early June of 2022 I went out into the Wasatch mountains in search of peace with my recent decision to leave the classroom. My choice of trail was one that I knew would be challenging (steep, rocky, and likely still snow-covered in spots). The trail would take me to a mountain lake that was to provide five-star beauty. After just over two hours of hiking hard I made it to the small lake, surrounded by mountains and rimmed in snow. I basked a bit. Then I noticed a steeper, rockier trail going up from the other side of the lake. I decided to take that trail and go beyond the lake. Despite already having several miles of steep climbing in my legs and this being my first significant mountain adventure above 9,000 feet of the summer, I kept going. About 30 minutes later I was rewarded with an incredible, panoramic view of the Wasatch mountains. I would have missed it if I had turned back. As I descended, I noticed several hikers reaching the lake and then turning back. They missed the best because they turned around early, not choosing the steeper, rockier trail to a spot that afforded intense beauty. A week later I went back with a small chair so I could sit and take in that view. It seemed like I could see forever and forever is a beautiful thing.

As the finish line of this project came into view, I knew that I needed to address the impact of COVID to provide a proper perspective of what lies ahead. I reached out to approximately 50 teachers in the spring of 2022. I had worked with each of these individuals at some point in my 40 years as an educator and each of them has contributed much to the profession. They are the ones who have taken the "steeper, rockier trail." Over two dozen of these individuals agreed to be interviewed as the 2021-22 school year finished. Just the fact that these teachers were willing to give me an hour (or more) of their time as they were finishing a draining stretch of months demonstrates their care and commitment. My career has provided the good fortune to sit with and discuss athletic training with Olympians, even world record holders, and discuss teaching and learning with state and national "teachers-of-the-year." I knew that bringing together the collective experiences and ideas from extraordinary teachers in 6 different states would infuse my work with inspiration and insights tempered with a strong dose of reality. I spent many hours in the summer of 2022 talking with teachers, summarizing their responses, looking for common themes and simply reflecting on their words. I was reminded that I have poured so much time, effort, and love into this writing project and I want to finish. This group of teachers each possesses a special brand of endurance which not only helped me recapture the faith that a message of endurance is both timely and essential but also helps frame the extreme challenges ahead.

Each interview allowed a chance to catch up and hear about what's been going on in the personal and professional lives of these teachers. I asked each teacher three questions (see below) and on the following pages I will share a summary of what I heard and how it impacts the teaching profession. Within their words exist not only some inspiration at a crucial time but also some actionable ideas that combined with the rest of the book provide a resource of replenishment.

Question 1: Can you share a story from your work with students when you felt a strong sense of reward or gained a little "victory", or you felt like "this is right where I belong"?

Question 2: Have you felt a sense of disappointment in your work as a classroom teacher? If so, what is the source of that disappointment?

Question 3: What do teachers need most right now? Or for the beginning teachers – what would make your work more meaningful?

Results from Question 1 – memorable moments and little victories

Hearing the best memories from 25 exceptional educators was an extremely uplifting experience. All these stories deserve to be told. I am humbled by my attempt to capture significant moments in the lives of teachers, especially teachers I care deeply about. I begin this section with a vignette that attempts to capture the essence of many of the teacher stories. Second, I will share one of the actual stories I heard, one of several that brought me to tears as I listened to the deep emotion from a caring educator. Finally, in reporting the results of question 1, I will share a summary of ideas and insights gained by collecting this data. It's been said that stories are "data with a soul" and the stories summarized here were good for my soul (and I hope they will prove for yours as well).

Vignette: Nobody in the class could stand Sam. He was emotionally immature and struggled in all subject areas. Some of his classmates called him "Stinky Sam" due to his poor personal hygiene. He just couldn't fit in or get along with anybody. It would have been easy for Sam's teacher to allow Sam to remain separated from his peers. After all, in group work and social interactions, Sam consistently caused distraction and disruption. Yet something about Sam stirred action from the teacher. Sam's teacher didn't give up or give into typical human reactions which might have allowed Sam to be more isolated, physically, and emotionally, from his classmates. She intentionally began interacting with Sam daily. These interactions included subtle attempts to learn what was important to Sam, helping him to articulate what he was thinking and feeling. For many weeks the interactions seemed to make little difference in Sam's behavior or effort. Yet sometimes they afforded an opportunity to laugh together or share a common personal experience. Occasionally the teacher would catch a glimpse of change in Sam's attitude or effort and would call home to report these positive encounters. The teacher discovered that Sam's parents didn't believe in Sam's ability to succeed but that fueled her desire to show Sam that someone did. Eventually Sam's performance began showing improvement and while good grades and proficiency with state standards were rarely achieved there was a significant amount of transformation in Sam. He showed an increased ability to sustain effort and focus. Though he did not become a class favorite in the eyes of his classmates, he did begin to interact more positively in some group settings. Months later Sam showed up after school with his school's yearbook asking for the teacher to sign it. As he left for the summer he said, "Thanks, you were like a mom to me."

The vignette above captures key elements from many of the stories that were shared with me during the teacher interviews conducted in the summer of 2022. I am convinced that teachers long to lead significant lives, yet significance cannot be imposed. Significance is created with others and once it is found it can be shared and deepened. There were several common themes uncovered in teacher responses to the first question but perhaps the most noteworthy is that these stories are rarely shared. Only two of the interviewed teachers had shared their reward story beyond a small personal circle, if at all. Connecting with students in a powerful way can weave together two hearts and two souls and is a lesson that endures. It becomes a way of life and promotes the desire to pass significance down to students and colleagues alike.

I believe that we all have gifts and talents. Brene Brown in her book *The Gifts of Imperfection* shared the thought that "when we don't use our talents to cultivate meaningful work, we struggle." When our work feels less than meaningful, we get "weighed down by feelings of emptiness, frustration, resentment, shame, disappointment, fear, and even grief." I think this is increasingly true in the current landscape of the teaching profession. When the work of teaching feels meaningful it helps a teacher come "alive" and helps them see beyond the inevitable challenges. During the interviews each teacher came "alive" when sharing their stories, yet it seems that opportunities to tell their stories are rare or non-existent. The little victories that teachers experience with their students need to be acknowledged, appreciated, even celebrated. When this happens consistently it helps them access "matters of the heart" and gives them a stronger sense of self within the prescriptions and mandates overwhelmingly found in the teaching profession. One teacher said, "it felt good to show this student who I truly am." Although the rewards described by these teachers were typically simple and intangible, it seemed to remind them that they were making a difference and "stir" a strong sense of gratitude.

In addition to uncovering the reality that teacher stories of reward are rarely shared there were three other noteworthy themes across the responses. It was evident that in nearly every case:

- Student issues which created the need for special attention were non-curricular. They were personal and highly emotional.
- The connection was built with an extra layer of communication.
- There seemed to be a supernaturalness in how the need was noticed and responded to by the teacher.

Often respondents could not provide a clear explanation of why they took on the challenge of trying to transform a student who seemed unreachable and unteachable. A typical response was something like, "They just seemed to need a little something extra." I think we must acknowledge that the attempts to make the teaching profession a competitive culture through testing, comparisons, and accountability measures often fail to produce excellence because those things are at odds with why teachers choose to become teachers. Experience tells me that most caring and committed teachers fear losing their students more than they fear losing their jobs. Their love for students runs deep and can change the course of life or a career. I think it's more than serendipity when a teacher notices a student's need and sees the worth and potential of the individual. Often, I have seen or felt a sense of the miraculous in the extent of impact that a teacher can have on a student.

Early in her teaching career Amy Brooks encountered a troubled student that would impact her development as a teacher like nothing else. Ms. Brooks, a former student of mine, now a teacher in Oklahoma, shared the thought that was my own almost 40 years ago. She said, "At the end of my first year I was going to quit." But then she encountered "Elena." This 13-year old girl was battling depression and "hiding" from others by turning up the music loud and pretending that nothing was wrong. Amy noticed and reached out for a conversation. Here is a compilation of Elena's own words captured in her essay titled - A Life-changing Seven-digit number. "…Evidently this was meant to be a private conversation because Mrs. Brooks moves us into the hallway. As I stand, I slide my watch down to hide the cuts that I regretted doing earlier that day. Why did I do that? I feel stupid but manage to pull myself together as the door closes with a click. I've thought this through and decided that if I had to tell someone about my depression, it'd be her. I feel like she'd listen with open ears and without judgment. I wonder for a second if she's noticed, and my palms sweat a bit. I snap out of it when she starts to talk. 'Elena, I've noticed that the topic of suicide has come up in conversation a lot and I'm concerned about you.' I shiver at the word suicide but stand strong and keep my head up. Mrs. Brooks continues, 'We care about you, and I know it's easy to joke about it, especially if it's crossed your mind.' It's crossed my mind a lot, I think to myself. And then Mrs. Brooks says words that I've never heard before, not even from my best friend, 'I'm here for you if you ever want to talk.' That last sentence gives us matching smiles. My heart melts with that smile and the smile stays. Thank you, I manage to say, swallowing my tears. I've never felt comfort like this, it's nice. I could sit down in the empty hallway and talk to her for hours. There's a long pause and I suspect that she's finished. I am lost for words, so I reach for the doorknob. 'And I'd like to give you my phone number, just in case you ever want to talk.' She finishes. She doesn't realize that I've thought about suicide more than once. I felt alone but now when I find myself hitting rock bottom, I have someone to talk to. Even if I chicken out and never call, I'll know that I'm no longer alone. We casually reenter the classroom and I wonder if she knows how much this means to me. I sit in a desk near hers and just smile. She hands me a yellow slip of paper with her name on it and seven digits, my smile grows larger. Later, I sit outside gripping the small yellow piece of paper tightly like I had been during my last class. This yellow piece of paper gives me hope and my heart fills with joy; maybe things will get better after all. I'm hopeful that something better is waiting for me at the finish line of this race to adulthood. I decided that I want to stick around to find out what good things await. I watch Ms. Brooks drive away after saying farewell. I can't help but wonder if she knows what she's just done: She saved my life."

In my conversation with the teacher, Amy Brooks, she indicated that the lesson learned with "Elena" helped her see past the overwhelming burden she felt as a beginning teacher. She said, "I realized that I love math, but it really is about relationships." That sentiment is often expressed in teacher preparation activities but it's not until it becomes real that it makes its way into the heart of a teacher. When teachers lead with their hearts their students feel it and respond. Sometimes the response is achingly slow. Yet the first steps of transformation while often small and unsteady are frequently instigated by (in Elena's words) "someone who cares." Amy discovered how to teach beyond the curriculum and helped Elena overwrite the labels of depression she owned with new labels, none more important than LOVED. As a teacher educator I have heard uncertainty from most novice teachers. I think the most crucial uncertainty to overcome in becoming a teacher lies in developing the confidence that you, the teacher, are uniquely positioned and qualified, to notice the various needs of your students, see past the labels placed on students, and respond in a way that helps each individual become their very best. This confidence can only be nurtured in a school environment where stories of impact, like the one above, are shared and valued. The opportunity to apply this confidence in classroom settings can only be created when we (in the words of two teachers from Wisconsin) "let teachers do what they are passionate about."

Results from Question 2 – Dealing with disappointment

Disappointment. Something I am intimately familiar with. It has always been there in the teaching profession. Teachers have always known disappointment is lurking when you pour yourself out for kids. After all, they are young and still developing. A classroom of young people includes the gamut of student types. There will be CAN'T, WON'T, easily distracted, unwilling, disagreeable, un-engageable, challenging, those that don't see relevance and let you know, and those that just can't believe that you, the teacher, or the lessons you provide lead to anything or anywhere that is worthwhile. Add to that children who come from homes with extreme poverty, addiction-addled parents, or no discipline and character building in the early years and it is inevitable that the job of teaching is pierced with disappointment. When asked this question one enthusiastic teacher from Colorado exclaimed, "It's really hard not to be!"

However, even though disappointment has always been "part of the job" in working with young people, it is more frequently collapsing into disillusionment. This collapse is being seen across our country. Sometimes it has been referred to as the "mass exodus" because teachers are leaving the profession in unprecedented numbers. I am concerned about that new reality in many parts of our country. Disappointment and disillusionment breed a discontentment within that makes one want to be somewhere else or be someone else. But it is the brokenness of those who stay that is most distressing for me. Some of the best teachers are being broken and the ability to replace them is getting more difficult. The teaching profession was already teetering. Many teachers were dealing with a quiet, inner anguish because of increased demands and decreasing rewards. The "tidal wave of trauma" that washed over us in the form of a pandemic, in the words of one educator in Colorado, has left teachers are "worn and torn." When we are disillusioned neither hope nor joy comes easily and a sense of "blankness" enters our lives.

Often during my time in higher education when sharing challenges faced by student teachers and their mentors I would be told "that's just anecdotal evidence." So, while this summary of teacher responses to a question about their experiences with disappointment lacks a strong scientific approach, I believe the voices of teachers that remain in the profession with a high level of care, concern, and commitment are the voices that need to be heard at this decisive moment in our country's history. I am reminded of a scene from the movie *Hoosiers*. In this culminating scene a basketball team from a small town is playing for the state championship against a much bigger school and seemingly unbeatable opponent. After falling far behind early in the game the team from the small town of Hickory had clawed their way back, tied the game and stole the ball to gain the final possession with 19 seconds left in the game. The coach calls a time out and gives them a play that appears to make sense but calls on the team to forego passing the ball to their star player, Jimmy. Immediately all the players turn their backs on the coach in disdain. He realizes that he has lost them and says ardently and repeatedly, "What's wrong with you?" He is met with silence until Jimmy looks him in the eyes and says, "I'll make it!" The team believed in Jimmy. Jimmy believed in himself. The coach found belief in his team. History was made.

I believe the voices of these teachers point to crucial issues that need to be acknowledged and addressed. More and more, children enter schools wringing with pain and disenchantment. Children have always started school incomplete but increasingly they lack the childhood experiences that are essential to having open, pliable minds and hearts that allow lessons of content and character to take root. Too often society has assumed that teachers will pick up the slack, work harder and carry children across the finish line, prepared for a successful life. This has become a huge burden on the hearts and lives of teachers.

There were four significant and consistent themes about disappointment revealed in conversations with participating teachers. I think it important to note that while tangible resources, like technology and curricular supports were mentioned, over 90% of responses addressed intangible issues.

The most frequent component of disappointment mentioned was in the realm of student interactions. It seems that one result of the COVID impact has been a decrease in student effort coupled with an increase in student rejection of deep engagement with ideas and activities. Often referred to as student apathy teachers are feeling increased disappointment in students' belief that their effort and engagement will lead to something worthwhile. Several early service teachers mentioned frustration that their own effort was not acknowledged or reciprocated. One Junior High teacher in Wisconsin indicated that many of her students expressed the attitude of "I can learn this later so why try hard now?" Another teacher, at the high school level, mentioned that combined with weak student effort, a constant message from the school's administration that says "just pass the students" feeds the voice of "It Doesn't Matter" that seems to have grown ever louder in the past two years. This kind of messaging from administration was another theme of disappointment and carries with it the likelihood of unempowering teachers. One first year teacher in Wisconsin shared an inner battle with uncertainty because of scant messaging from administration that was hard to understand and often difficult to accept.

Another indicator of the decline in student effort and engagement was an obvious deterioration in student interactions. Did the pandemic push young people into a cave of isolation where meaningful interaction did not or could not happen? I think there is no doubt that the vibrant conversations that help classrooms come alive have diminished, particularly at the secondary level. In our rush to cover all the topics that students missed during the past two years we are neglecting the opportunity for students to process and articulate important ideas. In the haste to return to "normal" are we disregarding the need for learning experiences to be meaningful and memorable?

During the pandemic, when long stretches of time saw schools in Utah fully online, I was asked to supervise practicum experiences for college students intending to become elementary teachers. This experience was comprised of me virtually observing my college student virtually watching (usually with minimal conversation) a small group of children listening or working. I sensed this was a poor substitute for my students and the students they were "working" with.

I fear that our desire to return to normal will result in schools doing things in impoverished ways in an attempt to capture what's been missed.

The second most common theme expressed by this cohort of resilient teachers produced much discouragement for me. As a life-long educator who has devoted much of his career to teacher support activities I found that nearly all the early-service teachers and several veteran teachers indicated that significant growth opportunities have either disappeared, become insubstantial or never been made available. Even when professional development activities were present several of the interviewees indicated that the time allotted for these activities was meager, even inappropriate. The result of insufficient growth opportunities seemed to lead to a decline in confidence in beginning teachers and a feeling of being stuck for experienced teachers. I fear "the stuck." Social psychologist, Alison Ledgerwood indicated that we need help and practice in moving out of stuck. Her research revealed that most people hold a fundamental view of the world that tilts to the negative and they stay stuck there. While teachers need opportunity to acknowledge and address the tough stuff they encounter during a typical week (sometimes called venting) they also need consistent and genuine opportunities to talk about the good stuff. Moving through trauma calls for processing the struggles but also requires opportunities to rediscover vision, hope and desire. Teachers need the space and time for this to happen. Residing in "the stuck" for the remainder of a career is not healthy for teachers nor the students they teach.

Conversations about disappointment with these caring educators contained a strong note of sadness. Many of these individuals shared feelings of shame in not being able to "do it all." Besides using words like overwhelmed and ashamed to describe how they often felt on the job I heard some teachers indicate that "it's hard to feel good about my work." Perhaps making the strong sense of disappointment with student effort even gloomier was captured by one veteran teacher's statement that with the necessity of lowered academic expectations for our students has come lowered expectations for student behavior. Inability to meet content standards is one thing (which is what teachers are experts in dealing with) but the loss of respect and dignity (something mentioned by nearly every participant) creates a chasm between what teaching CAN be and what teaching IS. Martin Luther King, Jr. said, "We must accept finite disappointment, but never lose infinite hope." For too many teachers AND many students hope is gone.

Results of question 3 – What teachers need

I began this project nearly a decade ago because I saw a need. That need has grown to an alarming level. In my conversations with teachers, I sought to uncover and understand what teachers need most, knowing that more than ever TEACHERS NEED HELP! Perhaps my own experiences in the classroom and in working with teachers in their classrooms helps me see clearly this intense need. Maybe it was hearing the heartache expressed by many teachers during the reign of COVID. Possibly it was the constant use of the word BURNOUT when describing the emotional and physical state of teachers across the country. Likely all these factors led me out of the classroom in May of 2022, compelling me to finish this collection of ideas, insights, and stories intended to provide the kind of help teachers need.

Simply put, teachers need support. Nearly every respondent used the word "support" to describe what they need and/or what the profession, as a whole, needs. Before describing the key aspects of teacher support called for by my cohort of teachers, I must share a crucial thought when considering teacher support.

Late in my time as a K-12 teacher, the principal in the building I worked in attempted to motivate the staff with a message that ended with "work smarter, not harder." At the time I remember feeling insulted because there was no doubt the entire staff was being asked to work harder. This administrator [soon to be on his way to the district office] thought he was showing compassion by hinting there was a way to avoid working harder while doing additional duties beyond what we were already doing.

As a coach, nearly every season, with about 4-5 weeks before the state tournament, I would give my athletes a short break. I told them to do as little as possible (don't do extra things with the additional time), get some extra sleep, enjoy themselves and return to practice a few days later ready to chase down our goals. While many of our competitors were logging extra miles and doing intense workouts my team was doing nothing. As a young coach I recognized that sometimes "no training" was the best training. The break replenished my runners. Not only did most athletes return refreshed physically, but their determination was renewed.

Jon Kabat-Zinn [known mostly for his work with mindfulness at the University of Massachusetts Medical School] indicated that "no agenda, non-doing time" is the cure for overwhelm and teachers are overwhelmed. A common need that I will call "reduce the more", a phrase coined by a young teacher in Wisconsin, showed up with the following pleas:

- "Let teachers do what they're passionate about." [teacher in Colorado]
- "Can't I just be a teacher?" [teacher in Oklahoma]
- "Things are so frantic there is no opportunity for depth." [teacher in Wisconsin]

- — "I wish we would embrace things that are sustainable." [teacher in Michigan]
- — "Everyone is so maxed out." [teacher educator in Montana]

It is true that camels are incredible endurance creatures possessing the ability to go long distances and for weeks without water. Yet if their reserves are over-tapped, they will sit down and go no further. We can't keep tapping the goodness of teachers. Already a significant number of teachers have "tapped out" and many others are overwhelmed. I think there is no doubt that living in a state of overwhelmed leads to emotional and mental depletion and for many classroom teachers' poor decision-making. This poor decision-making stirs up doubt for many and sometimes activates shame. Several respondents spoke about carrying a sense of shame home with them after a hectic day where they left the school building knowing they had missed an opportunity (or many opportunities) to address a need, or they had reacted poorly to a troubled or trouble-making student.

For those who think I am advocating for teachers to do "nothing." I am not. I only propose that intense effort interspersed with the habits of slowing down, examination, reflection and meaningful conversation provides a physical, mental, and emotional balance that is healthy in the long run. Giving teachers strategic and consistent mental rest is not promoting idleness but can deliver the necessary time to process the constant wave of change that is demanded of teachers. This is where teaching is extremely similar to distance running. When we find the right balance of work and recovery people will respond. I believe that when we provide opportunities for peoples' minds to wander they will become more attentive, more creative, and happier. I know that my best thinking often comes when it might appear I am not thinking at all.

I found it interesting and a bit troubling that the secondary teacher in the *60 minutes* episode mentioned earlier indicated that living with a constant sense of having to "be all over everything" led to her leaving. Now, with a new job, she discovered that she is not only "prized" in the world outside of education but has been able to find time for other pursuits. Many jobs are demanding but few jobs are dominated with the intensity of classroom teaching.

Besides getting help with the constant struggle of overwhelmed there were two clear and consistent themes of support that beg to be acknowledged and addressed. The first and most frequent plea for support came in the form of the nature of messages sent directly and indirectly to teachers. There is no doubt that many teachers are feeling unappreciated. As the pandemic began there was an initial and noticeable show of support for teachers. Teachers were recognized for the quality of instruction and care they gave to young people. Parents experienced first-hand the challenge of managing young people while leading their academic development. Many teachers worked hard to fill the gaps in the lives of their students and were recognized for their efforts. But then the pandemic lingered, and parents became frustrated and impatient. Pundits and politicians began using anti-teacher rhetoric to place blame on teachers for what was clearly lacking in our young people as they were preparing for college or the workforce.

I have witnessed and felt the results of the shame-culture that exists in many schools and communities. Rising above this is possible but it is taking a huge toll.

Increasingly teachers are feeling unvalued and disrespected. Many receive a "you have to do better" message from all stakeholders, sometimes even from students themselves. Over the past two years in classrooms across the country and in my interviews with teachers I heard the plea for respect and appreciation over and over. Somehow, we need to foster a replenishment plan for teachers that includes the kind of messaging that activates a sense of belief for teachers that their work matters and fortifies them for the challenges they face in the classroom.

The second theme that arose in my conversations with teachers as we considered what lies ahead, beyond the trauma of COVID, was teacher growth and development. Too often the teaching life is more demand & despair than reflection & guidance, more frantic than thoughtful, and teachers are more harried than helped. The remaining pages in the book you hold in your hands is all about the kind of environment, actions and practices that lead to teaching with endurance. I believe we can and must recapture the hearts of teachers, helping them endure a vulnerable time. I think the consistent disappointment and intense needs from even the best of teachers is a call for support from inside and outside the teaching profession. Teachers are looking for someone to come through for them. I hope the vision of growth and development you find on the pages ahead provides a breakthrough. As a runner, coach and teacher I found that breakthroughs only come after heartache. All of us have encountered heartache in the past few years, the breakthrough is just ahead.

COMPONENTS OF ENDURANCE

In endurance running the term "burnout" is used often to describe a state that includes a combination of physical lethargy with a lack of confidence in one's ability to overcome challenges or adversity. Both endeavors, running and teaching, are emotionally draining, physically demanding, and mentally taxing. Thus, it is not uncommon for a runner or a teacher to feel spent or burned out.

As a cross country coach near the end of a competitive season I would often hear "I'm just burned out," as an excuse for a poor performance. Resilient runners possess the ability to re-energize and perform at a high level after a stretch of self-doubt or weak training. During a school year it is not uncommon to hear a similar statement from a teacher to explain their lack of energy or wholehearted effort. Teachers face big challenges. Not only do they work in a highly demanding profession, but they must battle potentially toxic elements that are inevitable in schools.

Resilience for educators might be defined as the ability to adjust to varied situations and perform effectively in adverse conditions. Being a teacher requires spontaneous decision-making. They need a special kind of confidence that is *resilient* enough to deal with the ever-changing conditions and struggles of the classroom. Resilient teachers continually find a way to overcome the challenges and have an impact on young lives and this why I choose to use the term endurance to define the higher level of resilience crucial for teachers. The quote about endurance provided in this document indicates that not only does endurance allow you to bear and overcome adversity but to turn it into glory.

Unfortunately, there exists minimal research and attention in understanding of how to develop resilience in beginning teachers and there seems to be a cultural belief that with summers "off" teachers should be able to consistently recapture their resilience during their time "off." While time away from the intensity of the classroom is helpful it is only a small piece of the answer in the development of resilience. It seems that individuals have a choice in attaining resilience and cultivating responses to adversity which may be part of the solution to "burnout" and stagnation. There are some indications that one of the strongest resources in resilience advancement lies in the development of significant adult relationships. Resilience cannot be taught in a typical, transactional professional development event, it can, like the quality of courage be nurtured in a culture of trust. WE NEED SOME NEW HABITS that are realistic and sustainable in the current, highly demanding work of teaching. Positive thoughts and optimism can be powerful messages but for the bigger challenges that exist in the current state of the teaching profession we need a sense of reality in facing down the tough stuff. Facing the reality in many school situations is emotionally wrenching.

Following is a description relative to a resilient runner that I coached back in the 80's:

Despite being one of the best runners in the state, in two seasons of cross country he had only won one race, a low-key dual meet in Mt. Pleasant…but this was the State Finals, and his team was in the hunt for the Championship. His team was counting on him for a big performance…this team was more than just a group of runners, they had become best friends, had shared more in the past two years than most people do in a lifetime…he had to come through for them.

The weather was terrible…typical Michigan November weather, cold, raining, and incredibly muddy. Huddling with his team prior to the race, the desire flowed from each of them like a strong current of electricity…they felt nothing but a burning desire to win. The wind, the icy cold rain could not diminish the fire within them.

Knowing the mud was going to take its toll on the competition he concentrated on running a controlled early pace, so controlled that many competitors commented later how surprised they were to see him so far back in the pack at the mile mark…so controlled his coach was concerned that something was wrong…

On the double-loop course the one hill soon turned into a nearly impossible climb…the second time up saw many runners sliding back down or walking part of the hill, bent over and holding on with their hands…passing nearly 20 runners on the second time up this hill he realized he was in the top 10 and closing on the leaders. Over the last half-mile of the race while everybody else was struggling to "just get to the finish line", he ran the strongest 800 meters of his life, finally grabbing the lead with 400 meters to go and pulling away to a 5-second win. Later his coach commented that it looked like he was running a different race than everybody else…making every other runner look slow…he had a plan and stuck with it…he was STATE CHAMP!

Along the way to an individual championship this athlete had many frustrating and discouraging performances. So many times, he felt ready for a breakthrough performance yet come race time he "failed." What was it about this individual that allowed him to keep striving for perfection despite repeated failures? He was *resilient*. He was able to keep hope alive, in large part, because someone believed in him, which provided the impetus for belief and energy to remain when adversity and setbacks dominated his racing and training. He turned a season of adversity into a glorious moment, for himself, his coach and his team.

For this athlete, coaching required attention to matters of the heart. Conversations were more about inspiration than the science of running. Similarly, helping beginning teachers see how "experts" deal with adversity is critical in the development of belief in their own capacities to overcome. Even the best runners and teachers stumble, struggle, fail, and set aside the search for solutions until another, more convenient time (that rarely comes). Illuminating these moments and actions helps a novice realize that "failure" is neither unique nor a sign of incompetence; it is an opportunity to learn. For educators being able to continue wholeheartedly in the face of a variety of daunting uncertainties requires resilience. Nurturing resilience, a key component of endurance, needs to drive the professional development of beginning teachers. It is important to note that while resilience and its development can never be completely understood, we CAN learn to become resilient, and teachers CAN become more enduring.

During the COVID school year, starting in March of 2020, I got numerous calls from teachers in the field, individuals that were my former students or had worked with my students in practicum placements. They were struggling with the demands of their "new" required instructional strategies, disheartened because of the loss of connections with their students, and trying hard to feel hopeful about the future. Their pain was real, tears were common, and I found myself grieving their losses and frustrations. This vicarious grieving took a toll on me. I found myself wrestling with high-level discouragement. My own resilience was challenged by a new adversary, unlike anything I had ever encountered. I felt a small sense of fulfillment in being able to listen to and encourage these teachers in the field, but I felt little resilience against the adversity of a pandemic. I turned to these pages with a rekindled mission to provide lessons of endurance for others, and in so doing, recapture it for myself.

Teachers need endurance to become and remain teachers of impact. Endurance for a classroom teacher includes preparation in knowing what lies ahead - what is going to be faced in the classroom and outside the classroom. For an athlete, endurance is a toughened condition of the mind and body; for a teacher endurance is a preparedness of the mind **and** heart. Perhaps the most important aspect in the development of endurance is what is referred to in Harvard Business Review (2002) as "search for meaning." The dynamic of meaning making allows someone to build mental and emotional bridges from challenging and painful times to better times in the future. Victor Frankl in his book *Man's Search for Meaning* began developing a perspective on how to help individuals find meaning when locked in a Nazi "death camp." Calling his work "meaning therapy" Frankl said, "We must never forget that we may also find meaning in life even when confronted with a hopeless situation, when facing a fate that cannot be changed."

Several years ago, I shared some of the thoughts and ideas captured in this book with a small group of middle school teachers. I presented the idea that, as teachers, we are 100% responsible for the learning that takes place in our classrooms. After this statement, I paused and witnessed the inevitable rolling of the eyes, looks of disgust, and other negative body language. I then completed the idea with the "rest of the story." We also need to instill our students with the belief and accompanying actions that they are 100% responsible for the learning that takes place in the classroom.

This group of teachers appeared to have lost sight of purpose and meaning in their work. Their collective reaction to the first half of the responsibility statement, that I refer to in my own teaching as "the 200% rule", (from B. Wilkinson's *Law of the Learner*) revealed a loss. This loss, which I saw and heard often in my work with pre-service and in-service teachers, can best be described as a loss of the relentless pursuit of purposeful teaching: teaching for lasting change. With a loss of purpose, the work of teaching becomes less meaningful and fulfilling. Without meaning and fulfillment the spirit shrivels and with it, energy and vitality.

Teachers need to be prepared to endure disheartening stretches of time when it will be difficult to cling to the meaningfulness and energy necessary to impart lessons that are durable. The concepts presented in this section of the book include characteristics that need to be rooted out, illuminated, developed, and embraced for a teacher to continually endure and thrive with the challenges of making a positive difference in the lives and learning of children. While these qualities or virtues are often acknowledged as worthy, rarely are they acted upon as a part of professional development. They <u>can</u> be nurtured in a school environment where leaders value and attend to crucial aspects of personal and professional growth necessary to help individuals become teachers with endurance. Teaching is a highly emotional endeavor. When we attend to the intense emotions of teaching and develop the language to describe and discuss these emotions, we create a "portal to meaning-making, connection, healing, learning, and self-awareness" (Brown, 2021). These are things that need to be lived out in the day-to-day lives of teachers and school culture. On the pages ahead, I will share ideas of what those things are and how to make this happen.

COURAGE

*"Courage is the most important of all virtues because without courage, you
can't practice any other virtue consistently."* – Maya Angelou

Gus Lee, author and leadership consultant, defines courage as "utilizing all our brains, character, and spirit to advocate principles regardless of the odd, heedless of fear, apart from collateral impact, and independent of personal career needs." More than ever, it takes courage to become a teacher of impact. Teachers have become highly scrutinized, and often heavily criticized by parents, administrators, and politicians. To succeed at teaching, one must fail a little, nearly every day. This failure often comes in the form of rejection, the result of a culture that promotes questioning the expectations and activities in a classroom from parents, students, politicians, and administrators. Often this mistrust includes a degree of mean-spiritedness that Brene Brown (2012) referred to as "cruelty culture." It is a courageous act to consistently receive unjust criticism from outside sources and a lack of belief from the students within a classroom and remain fully committed and caring.

Recently I was reading a book summarizing the key ideas from Vince Lombardi's life and work in the football coaching profession. The book contained a picture in which Coach Lombardi is sharing an embrace with a player. The picture captured an authentic look of belief in the player's eyes. This kind of belief seems to be much rarer in a world where questions of method and motive abound, and often results in a school community lacking in trust. Experience informs me that most teachers begin their careers believing they are exceptionally qualified to provide just what students need, both in academics and in personal growth issues. This belief can fade and with that fading the courage to be innovative is lost.

As a coach of endurance runners, I knew the greatest component of confidence came from the belief that we had done more than anyone else to be prepared for the big race. Leading up to the biggest races I would remind them of their preparation. It is a good feeling to stand at the starting line with hundreds of competitors, look into the eyes of your team and see the light of courage shining. There is no doubt that this confidence in their training allowed the athletes to be more aware of all that goes on surrounding a competitive race, be more relaxed and ready to respond well, and be bolder with their in-race decisions.

Courage and commitment go hand in hand. It takes great courage to continue wholeheartedly towards the goal of impacting young lives when who you are and what you do are constantly questioned or criticized. When wholeheartedness is lost convictions are weakened. While many see a convicted teacher as rigid and unchanging, convictions provide stability and poise when encountering adversity or challenge. Like the endurance runner that needs courage to face the inevitable pain during a distance race, teachers need courage to stand tall for the things they believe in.

It takes courage to engage deeply and honestly, willingly and wholeheartedly, in the process of reflection and change within a community of professionals. It is within an environment of trust that courage is enhanced. A school culture containing educators who are living examples of people struggling for understanding and meaning provides great inspiration for students.

I have witnessed a disturbing trend in many schools. A growing expectation is for teachers to become compliant (rather than courageous). Compliance steals creativity and weakens courage. When teachers become implementers of someone else's good ideas (or worse, someone else's untested, unpracticed interpretation of good ideas) these ideas and resulting practices often fall short of success. When teachers become overly compliant, lacking the courage to question or challenge the latest "quick-fix" handed down to them, two things can come into play. First, the intended change or growth begins with a sense of uncertainty or distrust. Secondly, when teachers wait for direction, they fail to become instructional leaders and cannot grow as problem solvers and reflective practitioners.

A lack of courage was never clearer than during interviews for a study intended to reveal what aspects of mentoring were most important in the growth and development of novice teachers. When interviewing the mentors in this study I consistently discovered uncertainty in how to provide assigned novice teachers with the experiences and growth opportunities necessary for their development as teachers. Each mentor possessed vast experience and was considered a master teacher yet seemed paralyzed with the task of leading one individual. A typical response was captured with the following statement, frequently expressed by mentors in the study, "I wish they would tell us what to do."

Courage is necessary to overcome and override the limitations that are often placed on teachers. This development of courage is something that can be learned. It is an issue at the heart of school leadership and school culture. Barth (2001) stated that "it is the culture of the school that determines the achievement of teachers and students alike."

When teachers' lives and professional growth become limited to just individual classrooms the creation of a school culture as a community of learners remains out of reach.

Brene Brown in her book *Daring Greatly* (2012) shares a template for nurturing courage. When encountering failure and tough times she gave herself permission to feel hurt, "pissed off", shed tears, and be alone with this heartache for a time. But then she would talk through the failure and challenge with someone she trusted and loved, and this would allow her to move on, feeling "more courageous, more compassionate, more connected." I continue to believe that teachers have the grandest of opportunities to uncover treasures within young people. That uncovering takes hard work and hours of devotion and faith and focus and a constant recapturing of courage. Beginning teachers, just like the young runners I coached, need help with being courageous over and over again. Helping novice teachers cling to the belief that they have treasures hidden within them is a crucial part of teacher development because fear always shows up when one is trying to be creative or inspirational. This fear shows itself with uncertainty and doubt and often causes teachers to stay safe within the confines of ordinary.

I recently had a conversation with a former student. Ben is in his third year, teaching 7th grade mathematics and beginning work on a master's degree in Teaching & Learning. He spoke with great enthusiasm about his recent work in choosing a new math curriculum for his district. It seems that in allowing this novice teacher to investigate possibilities, share his findings, and make recommendations gave him permission to dig into his own beliefs about what it means to teach and learn mathematics but also helped him become more courageous. He indicated that this work (rarely given to a beginning teacher) helped him develop a "strong sense of confidence" and that it felt good to know that my district "believed in me."

Perhaps the story above provides some guidance for Teacher Development. Experience tells me that beginning teachers are often given tasks that ultimately feel trivial and meaningless. By "letting go" of an important curricular decision Ben's district showed faith in his ability to find the best option for students and teachers in his district. I suspect the results of this shared leaderships included a quality curriculum choice, higher confidence and loyalty in Ben's future work, and more opportunities for teachers to have a voice in the school district.

It seems that teachers are naturally good at encouraging but might need help with couraging. In her book *dare to lead* (2018), Brene Brown noted the importance developing the quality of courage. Yet, she indicated "we haven't made great progress in developing these skills in [others] because we don't dig into the humanity of this work – it's too messy." In becoming an ultramarathoner I needed to be intentional about the development of courage. I knew that in long endurance challenges I would have to face fear in many different forms. Encounters with wildlife (I've had scary ones with dogs, bears, moose, and rattlesnakes), being lost while on the brink of fatigue or dehydration, scaling mountains and cliffs with a broken-down body and cloudy mind, trudging through the dark on a rough, rocky trail where each step was uncertain, and coming up against the thought "I can't" were sometimes fear-producing experiences. I needed to practice and prepare to be courageous by putting myself in situations where I overcame fear and grasped the belief that "I can."

For teachers practicing and preparing to be courageous is critical teacher development. Living the teaching life has given me many wonderful moments of belonging, in my own classroom and with my colleagues in a school. Yet there were many moments when I needed to stand alone and do what I believed in. It took great courage to do something different and sometimes go "against" administrative dictums. Always these moments forced me to gather my courage and explain my decisions. Often, I was compelled to share my heart with another teacher or a leader in the district. Overcoming those kinds of vulnerable moments helped me be courageous enough to try new things in my classroom and help novice teachers find their best, creative self. Just the simple act of sharing an exciting idea for an upcoming lesson can be a practice in couraging. Too often teachers don't promote excitement and guard their hearts. This minimizes the chance for rejection but additionally minimizes potential opportunities for creativity, connection, and learning. As Brene (Brown) would say by minimizing the pain we minimize the joy.

"Courage starts with showing up and letting ourselves be seen. Every time we choose courage, we make everyone around us a little braver." – Brene Brown

HUMILITY

"Pride is concerned with who is right. Humility is concerned with what is right." – Ezra Taft Benson

Experience tells me that I must follow up the discussion of courage with a concept necessary for the development of enduring courage. Finding the ability to teach with endurance requires humility. Confidence and courage seem to go hand-in-hand, yet any discussion of courage should be tempered with attention to humility. Becoming a teacher of impact is a never-ending process, a constant pursuit of knowledge and know-how. Sometimes called life-long learning it is a determination to consistently figure out how to help a new group of students with an ever-changing and unique set of needs in the most impactful way.

It is a spirit of humility that spurs the becoming process as a never-ending pursuit. Wisdom is gained through a combination of relentless pursuit and a humble spirit, acknowledging the need to continually grow and learn. Teachers of impact "wring out" every bit of insight from experiences. They constantly are building a "mountain" of understanding and a practice that is hard to define with a list of catchphrases or best practices.

Sadly, this "mountain" seems to be "climbed" less often than ever before. Research exists that indicates individuals born after about 1982 exhibit an exaggerated sense of confidence. This results in a feeling of entitlement and limits the desire to learn and grow. In the previously mentioned study of mentoring practices, beginning teachers frequently responded with "I already do that," when discussing teaching practices or observing an experienced teacher teach a lesson. Rarely did observations lead to an examination of teacher actions. Novice teachers in the study believed they already knew how to teach effectively and missed key actions of master teachers that "cemented" the learning of students. I believe a lack of humility inhibits the growth of beginning teachers because a lack of deep examination along with rich conversations relative to teaching and learning is not developed as a consistent habit. Attend any Professional Development event and you will witness this limiting attitude of "I already know that." <u>Effective does not always lead to enduring.</u>

As a coach of endurance runners, I attempted to ignite the desire for a breakthrough performance. One of the many challenges in racing long distances is dealing with a high level of pain and discomfort. It becomes easy to remain "stuck" at a certain level because, quite frankly, it hurts. A runner must "dig deep" in order to push past the point when the mind says, "no more" and the body aches for relief. This "digging deep" requires moving past barriers that exist within all of us…possessing a hope and vision of performance that, while physically demanding provides great reward. Digging deep is a spirited attempt to give our very best. It is the ability to prepare our "inner spirit" to deliver a power beyond previous experiences. Digging deep is a concept at the "soul" level. When a runner is forced to dig into the core of their being and depths of their personal experience, they find soul. Digging deep delivers a capacity to do more than one ever thought possible.

I am reminded of a scene from the movie "Coach Carter" when the coach gets after his team because of the selfish, chest-thumping attitude that permeated the team after a victory. Rather than seeing team success as a result of collective effort, each individual began to believe that success happened because of what "I did."

Humble teachers never lose sight of the "we" instead of "me" in the classroom. They hold the belief they don't know it all and pass along a desire to constantly learn and grow. Humility is a combination of vision and mindset. It brings together the actions and beliefs that <u>all</u> can be successful and <u>all</u> need to and can continually learn and improve. These are lessons of endurance that add value to the lives of teachers and students alike.

ASPIRATION

There are strong indications that about 80% or more of teachers enter the profession with an inner desire to make a difference in society and in the lives of students. Yet without significant help and support this desire fades or even gets lost. When meaning and purpose are removed from an individual's work there is an inevitable loss of spirit. Parker Palmer in *Courage to Teach* (1998) indicated that the pace of change has teachers "snarled in complexities, confusions, and conflicts" and they become diminished. The current culture of public education with its attention to test scores, standards, and best practices, rarely attends to the question of why people teach, but it is in the search for answers to that question and the hopes and dreams of teachers where meaning and vitality are found.

Once I was working with a beginning teacher. She was facing the challenges of teaching mathematics to middle school students. As she expressed frustration in feeling overwhelmed with issues of classroom management combined with expectations to cover the district curriculum, she said loudly, "But I want atmosphere." This rookie teacher sensed that there is more to teaching than just filling a class period with curricular activities. Her "dream" was to have interested and lively students that interacted with the subject matter.

An educational landscape more focused on results with narrow metrics of success, along with accountability measures often accompanied with "or else" messages makes it easy for teachers to lose hope in a constricting spiral that leads to apathy or attrition. When one's work life is absorbed with things that leave one spent and disheartened it is incredibly difficult to fan the flame of desire to make a difference. The above-mentioned teacher's "dream" for a classroom atmosphere that made teaching rewarding included a constant frustration that the focus of teacher meetings continues to be schedules, systems, curriculum to be covered, and assessment data.

Teachers that remain in the profession typically fall into one of two categories: Pursuers or Pretenders. When the focus of work is solely the bottom line and rational systems to produce achievement, the pursuit for meaning, passion, and a sense of purpose is undermined. Schools need to continually confront questions of "What do we stand for?" and "What do we believe?" There is a loss of spirit when we create a school community in which everything seems to have a function, yet nothing possesses meaning.

It is in the wholehearted leaps of faith in trying something that you think might make a difference when the human spirit is thrust higher and farther. When school gatherings allow for, even intentionally instigate, the activation of hopes and dreams, when they are authentic and attuned to what matters most for students and teachers, and when they touch the heart & soul, teachers' imaginations are ignited and a constant flow of insights comes to life. One critical step in un-diminishing the teaching profession is to recapture significance in the work lives of teachers. Somehow, someway, schools need to constantly engage the dream of being better and best in the hearts and minds of teachers.

After 27 years in K-12 education I moved to an instructor's role in higher education. One difference in my work at the college level was immediately evident and highly motivating. I now had time to be thoughtful with my planning for class sessions. I believe that a first step in helping schools is the facilitation of actions like creating, inventing, and authoring in the work of teachers. Teachers have become compliant implementers of others' ideas and a substantial part of each day includes duties, supervision, monitoring, systems, data entry, and other time draining activities that often feel meaningless for a teacher with a dream of impacting young lives. Providing opportunities for teachers to think and act creatively feeds their spirit.

COMMITMENT

Numerous times throughout my 27 years in K-12 education I have heard an administrator say, "We will always do what's best for the kids." Rarely have I witnessed consistent action that demonstrates a strong commitment to this goal. I think there is no doubt that the intensity of constant change in the teaching profession has increased. Change is inevitable. We should constantly be searching for ways to improve and expand the impact of schooling for children. Yet there should be certain things we believe in and are committed to "no matter what."

Making a commitment is a decision to do something. The Latin of the word *decision* is literally "to cut off." Commitment requires cutting off all other options. One does not have to spend much time with veteran teachers to hear a strong, consistent voice of frustration with the continual faddisms that descend upon them nearly every school year. There is no doubt that the ever-changing expectations, mandates, and "flavor-of-the-year" priorities creates uncertainty, if not an intense distrust, in the teaching profession by teachers towards politicians and school leadership.

This has a huge impact on the teaching profession. Not only does it create a resistance to change in veteran teachers, but it negatively affects the professional growth of beginning teachers. The development of personal identity continues well into a person's twenties. Most young teachers are still wrestling with questions like "Who am I?" and "What do I stand for?" and "What matters to me?" The "quick-fix" landscape that currently exists in education, not only stunts the personal and professional growth of beginning teachers but it limits the potential for a school building to become a community where buy-in is a shared commitment from everyone. Buy-in leads to a powerful investment of time and heart; lack of buy-in leads to half-hearted efforts.

Attending to the latest fad typically results in a continual shifting of resources to things that come from outside the school, thus carrying with it uncertainty and mistrust. Every school contains a huge amount of influence but harnessing that influence is like harnessing an ocean. It is difficult to capture a school's influence and use it to create an authentic learning community. However, when a school is able to find something that unifies everyone commitment and persistence are enhanced.

In my book *It's Not About the Workouts: A Championship of the Soul* (2015), a compilation of ideas and stories relative to coaching teams of endurance runners, I penned the following passage nearly a decade ago:

> ***Stand for something.*** *There came a point when our team began to be called the CCC (which stood for Cross Country Cult). I believe this "name calling" was the result of outsiders seeing the commitment and connectedness we shared, and unable to find any in their own lives chose to sling "arrows" at us. I knew this bothered some individuals on our team, but I took great pride in the knowledge that our stand for close-knittedness was noticed.*

In the teaching and coaching professions, it has become increasingly difficult to stand for something. Teachers and coaches are expected to accommodate and differentiate their work, often allowing low effort and frail commitment to be part of the team or the classroom. This weakens the team connection and steals the deep meaning of having a united group with a common goal where everyone is expected to give their very best.

The teaching profession faces many challenges. Rather than problems, many of these challenges are really dilemmas, with no real solution. Yet these dilemmas constantly compel schools to determine what they stand for. When students believe strongly that the teacher or coach that leads them has their best interests in mind it is easier to follow, to commit, and to respond to challenges with great effort. The same is true for teachers in schools. When teachers know what they stand for, when what they believe in is at the forefront of their work, they become committed people. Committed people, when confronted with challenges, will wholeheartedly search for answers. Uncommitted people will search for an escape.

GRATITUDE

One of my most enduring memories as a runner followed one of the toughest races I have ever completed. The Massanutten Mountain Massacre in Virginia was 50 miles of rocky, mountainous terrain. The previous year I had gotten lost and eventually dropped out, but this particular year, both my best friend Keith and I had finished well. While waiting for our ride back to Keith's house we sat on a hillside with a bag of potato chips and some dip and talked about the race and life. As the sun dropped towards the horizon, after a draining day on a challenging course, we lingered. I remember having the thought, "There is nowhere else I want to be right now." A strong sense of gratitude gripped me as I sat and talked with my best friend after just conquering what to that point in my life had been my biggest physical challenge. I could have focused on my sore legs, my bloody feet, my rock-skinned shins, or the fatigue from 10 hours of competing on a difficult course. Instead, I embraced a memorable moment. I was with a friend in a beautiful spot watching the sun set, smiling, laughing, and yes, hurting. I had no deadlines, no expectations, no demands, and no distractions. I had just spent a full day doing what I loved and had overcome a challenge that just one year earlier had gotten the best of me. It was perfect!

Gratitude includes "coming back" to an experience or a moment, acknowledging what has happened, and who helped make it happen. Developing a grateful spirit is a continuous discipline and is not necessarily natural or instinctive. Yet in a school community it can be powerful when practiced well. Gratitude brings positive closure to effort and events. It helps teachers continually find optimistic reasons for the "why" of teaching.

Years after the gratitude event with a good friend and a bag of potato chips described above, I "escaped" the work world for a week, heading out-of-town as soon as my semester ended. I left behind all demands and details, yet I had much on my mind and heart as my 36ᵗʰ year in the profession came to a close. I knew I needed to work through some uncertainty so I could recapture the hope and passion that had defined most of my previous years in the profession. On May 23, 2019, I got one of those majestic moments where deep reflection helps access great clarity. I went to PJ Hoffmaster State Park near Muskegon, Michigan, just as it opened at 8AM. Because of a recent injury my workout was a planned hike on the sandy trails near Lake Michigan. I took my trekking poles with a plan to hike hard. An hour into my hike all the stuff that blocks reflection and clarity (stress, busy-ness, distractions) faded away. For the next hour it was just me and the trail…my mind was clear, my heart was open. What I "heard" and felt was something I knew but needed to recapture, a lesson I've learned over and over and over again. I can't run much YET, but I can walk. I am not in the mountains YET, but I am walking hills. I don't know the path ahead for me YET, but I know I will find it. I was grateful!

Capturing a sense of gratitude was so energizing and uplifting. I realized, over the preceding months, I had increasingly seen the inevitable disappointments and discouragement that come with wholehearted living and working. By its very nature gratitude is a lesson that needs to be relearned and renewed. A grateful spirit helps us deal with all the slights and frustrations inherent in the teacher's life. Without gratitude, passion doesn't get fed and hope fades. That hour with a clear mind and open heart in a beautiful place made all the difference. I recaptured a grateful spirit.

There is strong evidence that teachers, as a whole, are overwhelmed and restive. It is difficult to be grateful in this condition. When gratitude is lost the work of teachers is diminished. Without a grateful spirit teaching is reduced to a technical, highly managed and scrutinized process. It becomes "just a job." Frequently, when the focus of teaching rests on processes, systems, and measurements of proficiency, what really matters is missed. What really matters are those special moments, shared with a student, when a lesson or an experience impacts their life in a way that endures. Those "perfect" moments can be created or enhanced and when acknowledged in a heartfelt manner they help generate gratitude. William James, renowned psychologist, indicated that, "The deepest principal in human nature is the craving to be appreciated." A community that fills the need to be appreciated does more than recognize accomplishment, it develops a practice of gratitude.

In the Disney movie, The Rookie, about a high school teacher/coach (Jim Morris played by Dennis Quaid) there is a scene where Morris comes near the brink of quitting in the pursuit of his dream of pitching in the major leagues. As he wanders around in a discouraged state of mind he realizes (with help from a call home to his wife) that it is love for the game that has kept his dream alive and it is love for his team that prompted a second chance. He walks into his minor league locker room the next day, approaches a teammate, and says with wholehearted joy, "Today, we get to play baseball."

Teaching with endurance requires the development of gratitude practices. Daniel Coyle, in his book *The Culture Code* (2018), shares two stories of practices that promote gratitude. First, Gregg Popovich, coach of the NBA's San Antonio Spurs, at the end of every basketball season takes each of his players aside and thanks them for the opportunity to coach them. Coyle said the coach's exact words are: "Thank you for allowing me to coach you." Similarly, the second story involves repeated expressions of gratitude that Coyle uncovered at a Knowledge is Power Program (KIPP) school in Harlem, New York, where teachers thank one another over and over in a variety of ways. One particularly powerful thank you was sent from an 8th-grade math teacher to teachers at other grade levels because of continuously increasing math scores. After sharing the recent results, the teacher affirms that these results were from better teaching at ALL levels and the email ends with these words: "… so thanks for being great teachers who are pushing to get better each year. It's working!"

Sharing a message of "Thanks" seems easy and to many trivial, but it can be significant when practiced with fidelity. Most successful groups practice gratitude consistently. Why is a practice of gratitude so important? I suspect there are a variety of reasons to support this practice, but I believe the most powerful reason is that it affirms, acknowledges and strengthens the connection between human beings.

FORGIVING SPIRIT

Increases in transparency, accountability measures, and social media have placed teachers under intense scrutiny. This can produce a sense of being criticized on all fronts. I remember early in my career coming home from an evening session of Parent-Teacher Conferences. Even though I had many positive and productive conversations with caring parents it was the one negative conversation with a critical parent that weighed on me and kept me awake most of the night.

Any teacher who works to make a significant difference in the lives of students will face unjust criticism. Any teacher that attempts to create a lively and engaging learning environment will face voices that include "this is stupid!" or "when are we ever going to use this?" Students that will not or do not participate can crush the spirit of a teacher. It becomes difficult to hold onto a strong sense of meaning and commitment when criticism produces that voice within that says, "it doesn't matter."

A forgiving spirit helps a teacher be effective. When someone criticizes you unjustly this becomes your foremost thought and steals your focus and energy. The simple act of forgiveness allows a teacher to release the energy-draining thoughts of anger and resentment. This negative emotion can be replaced with a sense of hope with accompanying actions that help one hold onto the pursuit of impacting lives. The reality is that most people who act unjustly in a teacher's life hold no sense or conviction that they've done anything wrong. Waiting for them to ask for forgiveness or change their behavior does nothing but distract a teacher and drain their energy. The simple "secret" of developing a forgiving spirit can make all the difference in maintaining a perspective that each day provides grand opportunities instead of awaiting more criticism.

I was fortunate to learn this lesson in a powerful way early in my career. This true story is so meaningful to me that it still brings tears to my eyes even though it occurred over 30 years ago. I recently shared this story in a presentation at a state math conference in Green Lake, Wisconsin and it produced tears for one of the participants. I suspect that every classroom contains at least one "Scott" who begins as a harsh critic but when treated with love and forgiveness can be transformed into a person, even teacher, of impact.

I first met Scott when he was a sophomore in high school. I knew who he was during his freshman year but thought myself fortunate that he was not in my class and not on my team. Scott was a brawler, constantly in trouble, often from getting in a fight or challenging a teacher in the classroom. Most of the time he was the instigator. During fall pep assemblies in Scott's freshman year, I frequently got to speak for a few minutes or introduce my team to the school. Our team was successful, so this opportunity came often during the months of September and October. Scott would mock me from the stands, yelling negative comments about me or my team. I didn't want to get to know him. Fortunately, the season ended, and I avoided charging into the stands to confront his poor behavior. I felt a sense of relief that I did not have Scott in class that year. I sure didn't want to deal with his behavior in one of my classes. Yet, on the first day of the next school year, there he was in the back row of my third period Algebra II class.

I won't share all the details (and how difficult it was to stay patient and care about this student who had consistently mocked me in front of the entire school) but I worked hard to get to know Scott and forgive his past transgressions. Even though I mostly wanted to kick him out of class I tried everything in my power to help him overcome the anger raging within him. I eventually found out he came from a broken home where the father was an abusive alcoholic. It became easier to see past the bad behavior. Scott played football. He was skinny but tough. Because of that toughness I cautiously asked him to come out for the cross country team during his junior year. I could tell he was intrigued but he avoided the request. The football coaches told me that even though he weighed only 135 pounds he was one of the hardest hitters on the team. I suspect his anger fueled him. I knew that anger would eventually lead him astray and felt like distance running was a good fit. He did come out for the cross country team that fall. It was a bumpy "ride" but his desire to compete was an inferno and when eventually desire became disciplined and focused Scott became a star. During his junior season he never won a race but kept getting better and better, eventually earning All-State honors. Our team entered the State Finals his senior year undefeated and ranked #2 in the state. Scott had yet to win a significant race. On a cold, muddy November Saturday in 1988 Scott ran the race of his life. At the State Finals he placed first. He was a champion. He overcame extreme elements and won the most important race of his high school career. This helped him earn a scholarship to run college cross country and eventually led him into teaching and coaching. One of my greatest memories was from the 2001 State Championships when my boys' team and his girls' team (at a different school) each won their own state title. We both were named respective State of Michigan Coaches of the year. Scott's passion was noticed and resulted in him being named commencement speaker several times. One of his teammates once said to me, "you saved Scott's life; if you hadn't asked him to come out for the team, he would have ended up in jail." Seeing the potential in Scott has blessed my life immensely. I will never forget the incredible silence, how with no words spoken, love was expressed. Upon leaving his graduation open house in June of 1989 he followed me to the car, standing about 10 feet away, looking at me as I sat in the driver's seat with tears in my eyes, knowing that even though things would change, nothing could steal the connection we shared, the transformation he lived, the difference that was made in his life, my life, and the lives of dozens, maybe hundreds of young people.

Initially finding the ability to forgive Scott for his actions seemed impossible. The anger within him, directed at me and those I loved shaped a negative attitude towards Scott. I wanted him to hurt and pay for his unjust treatment of me. With reflection and effort, I was able to slowly see past the wounds he inflicted and develop a new perspective. I realized that I was harboring a deep well of resentment within that cast a dark cloud, not just on my attitude towards Scott, but to all aspects of my teaching. By nurturing a forgiving spirit towards Scott, I freed myself to pursue positive relationships with many students unencumbered by the weight of resentment or guarded by indifference.

I believe that we often wait for someone to ask for forgiveness, and we waste precious time imagining a confrontation or the other's demise. This is highly unproductive. Forgiveness, given silently and consistently (even when it doesn't feel like it's deserved) allows resentment to dissipate and a positive attitude to flourish. Teachers with endurance understand that criticism is part of the cost of becoming a teacher of impact.

Similarly, I have found that the forgiving spirit needed to be given to myself. There were many times when a miscalculation or poor judgement led to a mistake. I would then wallow in disgust or dismay and the disappointment in myself would lead me to choose to risk less, thus losing that creative and enthusiastic spark that was uniquely mine. Forgiveness is the touchstone of a teacher who begins each day anew and continually recaptures the ability to love and care for all students.

One of my first attempts at an ultramarathon that contained the dual challenges of long distance and extreme terrain was in the mountains of Virginia in the mid-1980's. Mentioned earlier, this was a race that I had attempted the previous year but dropped out after getting lost for about 30 minutes near the middle of the race (and then failing to capture the determination to finish). I was much more prepared this time but as in most endurance races there comes unexpected difficulties. In this event the unexpected difficulty was developing several blisters that eventually broke open, becoming painful and bloody. At an aid station near the 40 mile point in this 50-mile race, I had a nurse who was working the aid station examine and "doctor" my feet. I could tell by her reaction that she had never seen feet quite so "tore up." She advised me to stop. I didn't, after all, I was only 10 miles from the finish line.

I learned two things that served me well in future races. First, pack extra socks so your feet can stay dry, avoiding blisters that can turn bloody and painful. Secondly, if blisters still come, you can move past the pain because eventually they will numb out. This experience taught me important lessons of preparation and endurance. Eventually my feet developed calluses from years of friction and "abuse." My body produced calluses as an appropriate response to what they were being asked to do. These extra layers of skin helped prevent painful blisters in future races that had almost ended my race in Virginia. These days I rarely get blisters on my feet because of these calluses and preparation strategies I learned through trial and error.

For the most part calluses are a good thing, helping an endurance runner avoid the pain of blistered feet, but they can get ugly and gnarly. As a teacher, encounters with harsh judgement, criticism, and rejection they can easily build up a protective shield around the heart, creating an unfeeling, callused effect. Teachers need to remain a leader with heart as they encounter inevitable heartache in and out of the classroom. They need to know another's doubt, another's joy, another's loss, another's struggles and be able to respond with care, love and understanding. When a teacher's heart becomes "callused" they lose the ability to connect deeply with students and colleagues. The practice of renewing a soft and open heart through forgiveness is an important lesson of learning how to teach for the long haul, with endurance.

PASSION

I have been asked numerous times by students, colleagues, and athletes, "How can you be so fired up all the time?" The truth is that I'm not. Life, especially the teaching life, can turn into a mindless or spiritless journey filled with details and duties that make teaching feel insignificant. There are many demands and criticisms that "shout" at teachers to "just do this." Teachers often find themselves doing more and more yet enjoying the work of teaching less and less.

Beginning teachers, at some point, experience a loss of heart or at least a dullness of the spirit. Often this loss of zeal is unanticipated and alarming to them. Passion is a special energy that allows one to see beyond challenges to what can be and is absolutely a necessary quality of a teacher striving to impact young lives. Yet this passion can be lost. The deluge of data and messages telling teachers that they are failing produces "wounds" on the private world of a teacher. The heart becomes empty, starving for something or someone to help recapture the fuel that makes teaching the joy-filled endeavor it was at the beginning of a career. That fuel is passion.

Passion is a crucial factor in any school. Passion is a combination of desire and belief that one can be or do something unique, significant, or special. When a teacher loses passion there is no one to ignite the desire and beliefs of children, no one to believe in them, no one to make them feel special. In order to motivate someone, there must be sparks of energy and enthusiasm which are born from passion. A school with passionate teachers is an inferno of energy and enthusiasm which leaves its mark on the hearts and lives of children.

Recently, I spoke with a former student-athlete currently working in a service business. Her work with customers and colleagues alike has proved inspirational and she has been recognized for this inspiration. She shared with me that the most important lesson she learned while a high school student-athlete was the lesson of passion. This young lady who couldn't make the basketball team became a difference-maker for her cross country team, sharing a high level of passion with her teammates and coach. She understands that "People are like sticks of dynamite. The power is on the inside, but nothing happens until the fuse gets lit." Passion, not proficiency, is what lights the fuse for a young learner.

The graphic below summarizes four conditions that impact a teacher's passion (guided by Gordon MacDonald's writing about renewing spiritual passion). I think it is important to acknowledge that while passion is a matter of the heart, we can learn about passion, we can recognize the things that drain our passion, and schools can be a passionate place to work and learn, or not.

Emptiness which leads to self-doubt or negative thoughts

Deflated: when dreams, good ideas, and insights fade away or are torn apart by those with misguided motives

Loss of Passion

Dried-up: a condition where a lack of inspiration leads to teachers becoming withdrawn

Disheartened: when a teacher feels intimidated by the performance of others or just plain overwhelmed with the job of teaching.

Passion is crucial to the teaching profession. I can still remember getting to mile 60 in one of my first ultramarathons and feeling completely drained. The realization that I had 40 more miles to go left me feeling defeated. Great teaching requires that one pour all of themselves into the work of impacting lives. It means that teachers can become "poured out", emptied of that sense of heart that fuels their passion. This is a dilemma. The search for and renewal of passion is fertile ground for vital lessons of professional and personal growth.

That race mentioned above provided me an opportunity to learn an important lesson of endurance. Just after mile 60 I faced one of the steepest climbs on the course, with temperatures in the 80's and high humidity I sat down on a big rock, wrestling with the thought of "I CAN'T." Dropping out became a real possibility. I looked down the mountain, thinking that I could be back to the aid station I had recently passed in about 10 minutes and have my crew take me back to the hotel. Fortunately, I quickly realized that my crew would have left the aid station area on the way to the next check point, by the time I got there. (With a degree of resignation) I looked up the mountain and decided to keep going, convincing myself that I could drop out at the next aid station. However, the next 2 aid stations did not provide access for race crews. I was compelled to keep going. By the time I got to the next aid station that provided crew access I was approaching mile 85 (in the 100-mile race). I decided that I could finish the race. After all, I had "only" 15 miles to go! That race, early in my ultrarunning career, taught me something that has stuck with me in running and in life: even when you feel like you can't take another step, you can find it within yourself to keep going…and even when you feel worse than you ever have before there will be miles ahead of you where you can recapture desire, energy and joy.

The experience described above helped me develop a "just get to the next aid station" mentality. This allows me to embrace the knowledge that no matter how bad things are it won't be long until something appears and helps me re-energize. The dilemma for teachers is that you must experience emptiness, often. Yet, the charge for schools, school leaders and the teaching profession is that sometimes it takes becoming emptied out before you can experience being fully filled up. In schools if we value control, compliance, and data over passionate, heartfelt, unique and sometimes goofy lessons we lose something highly meaningful in the hearts, minds, and lives of children. While how to do this is addressed in the coming pages it is critical that schools be places where teachers recollect themselves, renewing or perhaps rediscovering the passion to make a difference in the lives of children. When a teacher's work consistently includes passionate leaps of faith, when they believe that they can create something or express something that makes a difference for a student it propels their spirit forward.

In my work with University of Wisconsin-Stevens Point (2014 – 2020), it was a School of Education tradition that on the Friday before graduation all soon-to-be teachers gather to be informed about the process of earning their credentials. But before that time of gaining information all supervisors of these student teachers are invited to share some words of wisdom. One spring, I almost didn't go. I wasn't feeling particularly worthy or wise. I was empty. Yet I knew and had *worked with many of the students that would be there, so at the last minute I decided to go, <u>for them</u>. I slipped into a corner of the auditorium just prior to the start of the meeting when Sara, a former student, yelled my name and ran down the steps to give me a hug and let me know that she had received her first teaching contract. Sara had been a student of mine in a math course for elementary majors. When she began in this course she did not particularly like math and had little confidence but for some reason I noticed something special about her and was able to light the fire of energy, enthusiasm, confidence and desire for her to help kids become "DO-ers" of mathematics. Together Sara and I made each other better. I helped her build confidence, while she helped me remember the lessons of enthusiasm and energy. That little interaction, on the steps of an auditorium, lasted only about 2 minutes, but for those precious 2 minutes everything else slipped away and we just reveled in sharing her joy and reconnecting. Her joy and gratitude filled me up. What a great way to end the academic year…and I almost missed it. It took being emptied in order to be filled. I think back to the morning prior to that wonderful 2 minutes and I can remember feeling negative and spent. I wanted to be "left alone." Figuratively, I was looking down the mountain and wanting to "drop out." I chose to climb, and it was worth it.*

"Make me empty, so I can be filled." – from a song by Sidewalk Prophets, *Keep Making Me*

HOPEFUL

Just as I thought I was done, I realized there was more to write. After a morning on a beautiful trail in the mountains of Colorado the inner voice that has vexed me throughout this writing project visited me in the dark. As I lay my head on the pillow, in the darkness the voice whispered, "Your work is not worthy. Your writing is crap. It doesn't matter to anyone." The voice of hopelessness attacked my desire to risk. Sharing my stories and beliefs about the profession I love is risky. Already I've faced rejection. Already I've had trusted friends "borrow" portions of this project for their own. The purpose of this project has always been to provide a message of hope and encouragement to teachers and for that reason I must find a way, muster the focus and energy, and hear the voice from an elementary teacher in Fruita, Colorado that approached me after a presentation of TwE, with tears rolling down her face she said, "Thanks, I needed to hear this today." [taken from a personal journal entry during August 2021]

As I approach the end of my professional career, I see clearly that a sense of hope is crucial for building endurance. A teacher's heart (at least this teacher's heart) gets broken over and over and over again. Trying to make a difference in the lives of students will frequently result in profound disappointment.

Early in my career, a wise man, a mentor of sorts, said to me, "Brad, you've chosen a career of teaching and coaching teenagers. I hate to tell you this, but they will let you down, <u>a lot</u>."

Holding onto the desire to make a difference when we encounter the disappointment of being let down by our students, colleagues, and administrators is hard. John Eldredge, in his book *Desire* (2007), said, "…the life we prize is always fading from view, and our hearts with it."

I can see now that part of what drives me, making me pour (too) much of myself into my work with students is my attempt to not let anybody down. Knowing the hurt of being let down pushes me to not do that to someone I love. I know the hardest part of being a teacher/coach early in my career as I started a family was a daily sense that no matter how hard I tried I was letting someone down…my students or my team or my own kids or my wife or my friends or my colleagues…

Hope is a source of desire and only when hopefulness is coursing through us can we hold onto the desire to push past disappointment and maintain a strong sense that "the best is yet ahead." When hope is gone teachers fail to capture the deep desire of impacting young lives. Instead of seeing a lesson as an enlivened opportunity for students to explore, reason, discuss, invent, and share ideas, it becomes, in the words of one of my student teachers, "I thought teaching was helping students put right answers on worksheets." An enlivened lesson leads to joy, for both students and teachers; completing worksheets with a bunch of right answers is an impoverished perspective of what a lesson can be.

Keeping alive the vision of a lesson that brings joy (versus one that produces drudgery) is central for the hopeful teacher. A hopeful teacher sees each student, each class, each lesson, as an opportunity. A hopeless teacher views a lesson as something to get through and misses the opportunities to turn "I can't" into "I can".

There are moments when the various components teaching come together and it feels highly uplifting, like it is meant to be. We must continually learn the lessons these moments provide or hope gets lost. When hope is lost it gets replaced with something else.

This past July I taught a Math Ed course for graduate students in Elementary Education. We had eight 2½-hour class sessions that were to "cover" all math topics required of Elementary teachers. An impossible task! I was fortunate. While I began the short summer semester somewhat reluctant to teach during the precious summer months where I typically strive to renew my passion for teaching, I found myself looking forward to each class session. My students were eager, enthusiastic, and willing. As the next-to-last class session was ending I risked asking a question of my students that had the potential to produce rejection or indifference. Before wrapping up for the day, I looked my students in the eyes and asked, "So, did you encounter anything surprising this semester?" After a moment of silence, one of my students, with tears brimming in her eyes, shared her fears of taking a math class and having others see her as "stupid." In a clear, sincere voice she indicated the surprise this semester was that she "enjoyed" math and had begun to "believe that I can teach mathematics to kids in way that helps them learn." This was a rewarding moment for me. I saw a transformed perspective on what it means to teach. I heard courage as she shared this with me and her classmates. I witnessed the building of hopefulness that good things lie ahead in her future classroom. Only by risking did I instigate a meaningful moment for my student and myself. It felt good to know that work we did together was more than "covering concepts", a lot more.

When hope is lost, desire is weakened. As teachers when our desire is reduced, shrunk from engaging episodes of challenge and adventure to requirements of completion and correctness, a spirit of indifference or even resentment takes over. I have seen this too often, particularly at the secondary level, hearing teachers blame students for a lack of understanding, sometimes saying the dreaded words, "It doesn't matter what I do, they won't get it." I will admit the extreme challenge of holding onto the belief that,

- – each student has something unique and special within,
- – each lesson is an exciting opportunity,
- – I am uniquely qualified to provide just the right stuff to bring out the best in my students, and
- – I can produce in my students a belief in me that I have their best interests in mind and heart.

Often, I wrestle with the nagging feeling that things are supposed to be MORE…more heartfelt, more inspiring, more joyful, more lasting. The challenge for the Teacher with Endurance is to pursue heartfelt, inspiring, joyful, and lasting moments, while frequently encountering disappointment. Teachers with Endurance move beyond disappointment. Teachers without endurance give up the pursuit and dismiss or deny disappointment.

I lost a running companion once. After many months of sharing our weekend "long run" on a beautiful trail somewhere outside the city limits, he chose to stay close to home and run multiple laps around the streets of his neighborhood. He told me he didn't want to take the time to drive out of town or seek new places to run because "I just want to get my workout done."

I will confess that not every long run results in beauty and adventure, but some do. I also acknowledge that not every lesson I teach is highly inspiring, but some are. I know that in the constant rekindling of the desire to create meaningful moments I capture the hope that each of my students can become the kind of teacher that is memorable for their students.

CREATING A CULTURE OF ENDURANCE

I recently read an article that summarized research regarding "good teachers." It seems that the good teachers in the study all possessed 3 seemingly intangible qualities. Two of these qualities could be summarized with one word: belief. It seems that teachers find a higher level of success when they express and demonstrate a belief that all students can learn and achieve and help students believe that they can find consistent success. Schools face a crisis of belief. The past few decades, in the name of achievement and reform, schools have become institutions that are mostly sterilized of faith and hope. This is a tremendous loss because without the human/spiritual components of faith and hope the work of teaching and the learning for students loses meaning. Below is a portion of an essay I once wrote for a local newspaper.

When students believe strongly that the teacher or coach that leads them has their best interests in mind it is easier to follow, to commit, and respond to challenge with great effort. Teachers that capture this belief have a greater opportunity to help students learn lessons that stick and coaches that capture belief are more able to help athletes find breakthrough performances.

I am fortunate to have experienced the POWER OF BELIEF. I am so grateful to have shared it with a many young men and women over the past few years. I know what it means to really believe. I finally understand that belief is so much more than knowledge. BELIEF is felt. BELIEF spurs action and prompts commitment. BELIEF creates a willingness to hurt, and the pain given in sincere belief cleanses and strengthens the heart...providing the ability to give more. BELIEF makes perseverance a way of life. BELIEF makes the impossible seem achievable. For a runner BELIEF keeps the vision of the finish line bright and alive. BELIEF gives purpose. BELIEF adds meaning to life.

My work with k-12 educators indicates that the power of belief is too often absent or lost. The current culture in schools is highly questioning of teachers and coaches. When a beginning teacher tells me of difficult parent interactions, they relate that it often begins with something like, "my student is struggling, what are YOU doing wrong?" When a teacher or coach is questioned in a visible or negative fashion it creates doubt in the minds of young people. Doubt is a cancer of the mind and heart that clouds the bright light of belief. When we try to protect our children from the lessons of hard work and discipline, trying to prevent the pain of failure, we rob children of opportunities to learn and grow. It is in the response to pain or failure that the course of our life is set. Seeing beyond past setbacks and failures and believing that the best is yet to come is a powerful way to live.

Building a true team involves the incredible challenge of rooting out selfishness. This process is painful and takes a great commitment by a coach, the athletes, and the parents. If belief is present, a connection that runs through the team is developed. This connection makes each person better, stronger, and the results can be significant. Yet, too often, that experience remains unattainable because missing is the belief and support that a team needs as its foundation. I have witnessed the results of this...I have seen this pain...I have observed the shallow commitment when belief is absent.

BUT I know the power that can be unleashed when belief is present. When belief becomes the lifeblood of a team, that connection creates a formidable current that pours out determination, focus, a will to go on, desire, and yes, love…and that is the greatest achievement in sport.

Schools face huge challenges. Perhaps the biggest of these challenges lies in the loss of belief. Many teachers have lost the belief (or it is easily eroded) that their work matters; the public has lost their belief that teachers have their children's best interests in mind; students have mostly lost their belief that schooling is relevant to them. Teaching and learning in the U.S. needs rescuing and that rescue begins by creating a culture where belief is instilled, cultivated, and valued.

RESCUING SCHOOLS – IGNITING THE POWER OF BELIEF

Bad weather pushed the final round of the 2015 British Open to Monday and the drama unfolding at St. Andrews Golf Course in England lured me in…I had to watch! The eventual winner, Zach Johnson, finished about an hour before the final pairings that included the third-round leaders. Zach played magnificently and made a long birdie putt on the 18th hole that proved crucial for him. What I will remember most about Zach's effort are three things. First, I will remember his intense focus during the final round. Golf requires "nerves of steel" with so much on the line and one small mistake often being the difference. Zach displayed an ability to rise above the distractions and perform at the highest level in his sport. Second, the pure joy he displayed in his accomplishment and the number of fellow competitors who shared in his joy. Finally, what I will remember most about the event, one of the biggest events of the year in sports, happened as Zach walked away from the 18th green towards the building where he would have to sign his scorecard to authenticate his score. He got part-way there and bent over, unable to go on for a few minutes. He was spent. Golfing 18 holes does take physical effort but Zach's inability to go on occurred because he had just completed an "all out" effort over 5 days and it took a heavy toll, much of it emotional. For a few minutes he felt like he could not go on…but he did, eventually winning the championship after a 4-hole playoff.

Similarly, teachers who teach with love, passion, and commitment often become spent, disillusioned, or discouraged and feel like they can't go on. The New Teacher Project (TNTP) in a report summarizing what great teachers think about their profession indicated a love/hate relationship. These "irreplaceable" teachers continue to cherish opportunities to impact young lives but feel "beaten down" by many aspects of the job. Teaching, too often, is like "sailing into the wind." Somehow, we need to lift up the spirit of the teaching profession and replace the climate of uncertainty and frustration with a climate of hope and possibility.

Currently, billions of dollars are spent for professional development activities and teacher improvement in the United States. There is strong evidence that despite this huge investment most teachers do not improve from year to year and even when teachers do improve, there are no clear indications of why they improve. However, it does seem certain that teacher growth is a highly individualized process, one that is often oversimplified, resulting in weak attempts at providing a list of best practices. Teachers are bombarded with "help" usually with a label of professional development, yet rarely does it actually help them in the pursuit of excellence and fulfillment.

People thrive under certain conditions. Creating the conditions in which teachers can thrive requires a reformation. The reformation of the teaching profession demands reestablishing some things that have been lost, renewing commitment to things that we know are vital for the profession, and creating a culture that fully restores meaning, purpose, and reward to the profession. Following is a list of principles that I maintain can help rescue the teaching profession from the malaise that all too often seems to invade schools and the work of teachers, thus preventing positive change efforts or recapturing of things done well. I have witnessed or experienced all of these principles but also observed and felt the empty atmosphere in schools where they are missing. These principles revolve around the concept of culture and as Louis Gerstner (highly regarded CEO) once said, "culture is not part of the game, it is the game."

This list of principles to guide school culture comes with a caution. It is not a "just do this" recipe for creating a culture. Education has become a profession of rapid change, often without a thoughtful approach. New teachers struggle to develop what they stand for which results in weak or misguided commitment. The following list is a compilation of ideas from a lifetime of being around teams and groups in schools. The principles presented here are intended to shed light on practices of schools or academic teams that seem to set them apart from most and helped the group rise above dissatisfaction and overcome many of the intense challenges that exist for teachers and leaders in the profession. It is my belief when these principles are implemented with a high degree of intentionality and fidelity it allows educators to embrace wholeheartedness and "when fully applied in any team situation these principles can lift performance and add meaning to the endeavor" of impacting young lives (Kahrs, 2015).

PRINCIPLE 1: IT'S ALL LEADERSHIP, BABY!

Early in my teaching/coaching career, the principal at the high school I worked in, always at work early in the morning, would see me enter the building the morning after a cross country competition. He would always ask how we did and was sincerely interested in how the athletes performed but also how I felt about it. Fortunately, the team I coached won many meets and his response to my description of the team's success was always the same, "It's all leadership, baby!" This response was intended to affirm my hard work and his belief that in sports the coach is the one that creates the culture that leads to victory.

There is no doubt about the importance of leadership in any organization. However, increasingly in schools, leadership has become more about position and metrics rather than about culture and people. When leaders value and focus on control and processes they often create resentment because it becomes evident that what they are about is getting people to do what they want in order to further their own agenda or enhance their career. Schools need leaders that are a living mission statement for a school; leaders that instead of creating resentment inspire people to do more, try harder, find joy in the effort, and bring people of diverse backgrounds and experiences together with a common purpose.

I believe that many public schools have mostly lost their way. School leadership plays a critical role in restoring a balance of excellence and meaning. The single biggest factor in that restoration requires a profound change in how school leaders view their roles (Deal & Peterson, 2009). For decades now the bureaucracy of schooling has thwarted the kind of leadership that is needed. Sergiovanni (2005) indicated that many schools allow management of structure, process and control of behavior rule over symbolic and cultural components. In the human endeavor of teaching young people, the construction of an environment of meaning and commitment allows the leader to bind people together. This connection requires equal parts intellectual concerns, methods & strategies, and inspiration.

During the data collection phase of a study intended to root out mentoring practices that enhance the professional development of beginning teachers, I found something about leadership that I thought was particularly enlightening. In most schools, teachers, mentors and mentees alike, used the word "they" to describe building or district administration. Only one building revealed teachers that used a first name when describing the building leader. When digging a little deeper, it might not be surprising that this administrator was the only one interested in qualitative data uncovered in the study that was pertinent to school leadership. It was evident that this leader was able to instill a "we" attitude in his building.

In today's school cultures, often containing a punitive environment because of accountability strategies, leaders must be "overcomers." The rapidity of change and ever-increasing list of demands can create a culture of resistance, negativity, or bitterness. I believe that the rapid change in k-12 schools often results in teachers losing trust in their building leader. They see that "what we stand for" changes from year to year and with that change teachers stop trusting mission statements, commitments, and promises. The replacement for trust is complacency, cynicism, bitterness, and attrition.

The early part of my career was spent teaching and coaching at a rural high school in Michigan. When I began, the culture of the school was one of pride and teamwork. However, my last years at this school saw the atmosphere became increasingly negative. School spirit and togetherness was replaced with a sense that everyone was working in disconnected silos. A deep commitment to doing what's best for kids was replaced with, at best going through the motions and at worst open hostility that drained energy and eliminated productive conversations. I remember the constant gossip, sniping, and toxic whisperings between staff in the hallways. At one staff meeting, a veteran teacher illustrated the attitude of many in a response to a group effort attempting to gain consensus on a school issue, "It doesn't matter what you decide, I won't do it."

Looking back on this incident it is disturbing to realize how quickly a positive culture turned toxic. It seems evident that school culture can decline rapidly. While building a positive culture often takes years, a negative culture can take over in a matter of months or even weeks. In this case, I believe the staff became overwhelmed and then embittered with the amount of change, especially in the school's leadership. Some teachers to avoid becoming bitter began closing their doors to shut out the negativity and worked in isolation. (I was one of those teachers.) When a school's teaching staff begins working in isolation people become detached and commitment wanes. Combined with a difficult mid-year move to a new building, the "revolving door" of leadership had sapped the strong sense of significance from a group of dedicated people. Soon after this incident I chose to leave. I remember referring to the school, now housed in a new spectacular building as a "dungeon" of bitterness.

Perhaps the most important role of a school leader is to instigate or renew belief. When a school is dominated with people that possess a strong sense of "I can" they become part of a team that believes in each other. Believing that your colleagues will do their best for you results in the will to do your best for them. With that mutual belief the foundation of a powerful culture is laid. When a team believes that their leader will always do what's best for the team, even when difficult circumstances are present, commitment and loyalty are strengthened and a culture of consistently overcoming challenges reigns. School leaders, that believe in the importance of culture and act accordingly, help empower teachers. With that empowerment comes discretion, creativity, sense of support, determination, and lasting commitment to constantly impact lives for the better.

PRINCIPLE 2: WE WILL HAVE CONVERSATIONS THAT MATTER

Authentic conversations can promote reflection, create reform, and inspire effort. Conversations in schools are often stifled, narrowly focused, and shallow. For adults, knowledge creation is usually a social process and yet interactions in schools are typically described as "on the fly" or stilted and frequently come with requirements of focusing on assessment data.

This reality can be particularly suffocating relative to building a culture that unlocks the door to commitment and excellence. In fact, when the level of conversation is consistently repressive the professional growth of beginning teachers is stunted. A previously mentioned research study of the relationships of mentors and beginning teachers in K-12 schools revealed that interactions were mostly "just in passing" and dwindled considerably after the initial introductory phase. This reality left mentors confused with their role and novice teachers uncertain about issues of professional development.

One troubling challenge in any organization is that when there is a gap in meaningful communication it gets filled with negativity. School leaders have the opportunity to become a significant element in the personal and professional growth of teachers and build a positive school culture when they model conversations of depth. These conversations don't just happen. They need to be intentional and consistent and in the busy-ness of schools it is difficult for building leaders to capture a practice of conversations that matter. The two short stories below illuminate the challenge of finding pockets of meaningful talk in a busy school day.

1 - A high school principal became convinced that consistently setting aside the first hour of each school day for talking with staff would make a big difference. He had a plan. Rather than let his day be ruled by what often amounted to trivial details he would start each day with a conversation intended to develop a stronger connection to his staff. He would begin the plan by focusing on those teachers he saw as leaders in his building, hoping that the plan would trickle down through the ranks. He was committed to the plan. The plan lasted 1 day. The intensity of problems and demands circumvented the belief that his role as building leader should include, as the highest priority, the development of meaningful conversations.

2 - A small group of 7th grade teachers, referred to as a Professional Learning Community (PLC), met weekly. This group was comprised mostly of veteran teachers with a deep commitment to children and the school. Their meetings were dominated with talk about weekly schedules, behavior problems, and feigned analysis of achievement data. For weeks there were subtle expressions of frustration that conversations were stuck in the shallow and trivial. Finally, it was determined that they take their meeting time "on the road" and in a new venue spend time discussing issues that were troubling but never seemed to be discussed or addressed. They checked out the school van, drove a few miles to one of the teacher's houses with a plan to sit out on the patio and "just" talk. For five full minutes this group of dedicated teachers started talking with energy and passion until a call from the school's secretary ordered them back to school so a small group of students could be transported to the local swimming pool.

Even with good intentions and obvious need conversations in schools are dominated with talking and being talked at, dealing with circumstances, problems, and issues that are often trivial. Barth (2001) in *Learning By Heart* shared the thought that authentic conversations in schools provide powerful "survival strength." Endurance is enhanced when teachers learn and practice reflection, where they are able to step and back see the challenges of teaching for what they are – and what they are not.

The practice of conversations is the key that unlocks the door to high-quality professional development. I share two insights from a past of pursuing understanding in this area: sometimes as a presenter, sometimes as a mentor, sometimes as a researcher, but all times as a learner. First, at a National Council of Supervisors of Mathematics (NCSM) conference a few years ago the keynote speaker said, "If we're going to solve the problems, we face in our profession then we need to recapture some of the things that we've lost." Second, in earning a doctorate in education late in life I completed my dissertation in 2011. This project, the hardest thing I've ever done, required me to spend dozens of hours interviewing teachers, mentors and mentees, in order to determine what is most important for beginning teachers relative to their growth and development. I was able to uncover several important realities for most beginning teachers and their mentors. Perhaps the most crucial findings were (a) beginning teachers start with a yearning for feedback and guidance yet rarely are they prepared for how to seek, find, and utilize feedback. They seek conversations of depth and meaning BUT in our busy, frenetic world this rarely happens. Communication is typically rushed and brief or through email, and (b) the issues that challenge novice teachers right out of the gate are rarely addressed in a meaningful way.

In the well-read book *Good to Great*, author Jim Collins shared the *Stockdale Paradox*. Named after Admiral Jim Stockdale, a prisoner of war in Vietnam from 1965 to 1973 and tortured more than 20 times, his story sheds light on how prisoners survive physical and emotional torment. (And maybe provide an important insight for one way we can help provide the kind of professional development that our schools need.) Stockdale indicated that surprisingly the Prisoners of War (POW's) that didn't make it home were the optimists. The optimists began their imprisonment believing that it would be over soon and then it would go on and on and on. Eventually disappointment after disappointment after disappointment led to a loss of hope. Stockdale indicated that the optimists, "died with a broken heart." Collins records Stockdale's words, and this is the lesson that we need to apply and practice with beginning teachers, "You must never confuse faith (belief) that you will prevail in the end – which we can never afford to lose – with the discipline to confront the most brutal facts of your current reality, whatever they might be."

In our profession there exist some incredible challenges. Beginning teachers often become frustrated, disappointed and discouraged, rarely getting the opportunity to work through and articulate the reality that the biggest challenges early in a career lie in the emotional realm. If we are honest there is a lot of heartache in store for a novice teacher. When this acknowledged and worked through with a trusted colleague it lays a foundation for building confidence and belief that "no matter what I can provide the instruction for this group of students that WILL make a difference." If we develop an intention and consistency of addressing the little things that eventually become HUGE things, we create a culture of "we all take responsibility for both dreaming and reality-checking those dreams and facts." When we deny our stories of struggle, they own us and drive our behavior, emotions, thinking and ability to lead in the classroom and out. When we own our stories, work through them, and overcome them, we develop the confidence and hope that helps build endurance.

The nature of our conversations determines, to a large extent, the culture in our schools and this culture, in large part determines the depth and meaning of the learning that takes place. Orchestrating meaningful conversations is a crucial component of professional growth that too often goes unattended. We are ALL responsible for the culture that defines who WE are.

PRINCIPLE 3: WE WILL CAPTURE SIGNIFICANT MOMENTS

A teacher in his third year was sitting at a staff meeting prior to the start of the school's second semester. He had his class lists and as he sat half-listening, a veteran teacher leaned over and in laughter said, "Oh man, you've got Max Burnes this semester! He is the worst behaved student I've ever had." The veteran teacher, highly regarded, had been teaching for 30 years. The third-year teacher had the thought, "I am not going to fight a semester-long battle with behavior." He developed a strategy to treat this potential troublemaker like a gifted individual. On the very first day he greeted the student at the door, asked for personal information, and requested Max's help in getting the class going. All semester he treated Max (considered by all others to be a weak student) like a co-teacher. Max assisted with handing out papers, helped students with difficulties in their work, and talked with the teacher about what was going to happen the next day. The novice teacher encountered no behavior problems with Max for a full semester. The teacher sensed that this experience was significant but shared it with no one (until years later). There was no venue to share. I was this teacher. The year was 1987. This experience was one of the most significant moments in my early years of teaching, and yet it was left unspoken for years. As I look back, I realize that many good ideas and practices failed to take root in my teaching because I never articulated my experiences, the successes and the failures.

People yearn for significance. This inner desire is strong in individuals that choose to enter the teaching profession and strive to make a difference with their work. Many teachers, at the beginning of a career, have chosen meaning over monetary compensation. Yet over time, disheartened with the intensity of demands and change, the pursuit of meaning fades. A school culture that finds a way to consistently renew meaning in the hearts and minds of teachers allows the work and sacrifice it takes to feel rewarding.

Important breakthroughs and significant moments in the classroom need to explicitly revealed. Not only does this provide reminders of why teaching is a rewarding profession, but it helps teachers sustain the energy and commitment it takes to impact the lives of young people. "Good results" or data cannot be the <u>sole</u> focus of staff meetings. When this happens a Professional Learning Community (PLC) is nothing more than a process that holds little reward and thus, little meaning. Leaders play an important role in collecting, sharing, and reviving stories and moments of significance.

PRINCIPLE 4: WE WILL BUILD A CULTURE OF MENTORING

Mentoring, as professional development has been shown to provide effective support to novice teachers, but mentoring practices vary widely and the components of mentoring that make it successful remain difficult to define. This has resulted in a lack of clarity in the role that mentoring plays in schools and the growth and development of beginning teachers (Kahrs, 2011). While teachers enter the profession incomplete and most schools acknowledge the need to support and assist in their growth and development, these efforts often fail. The study of mentoring cited above explored mentoring relationships to determine what aspects of mentoring seemed to be most helpful in the growth and development of new teachers.

It seems evident that schools with a culture of mentoring are more successful in retaining beginning teachers and in helping them move to effective and efficient practices in the classroom. So, what does it mean to possess a culture of mentoring?

Schools with a culture of mentoring exhibit reflective practices with supports in place to enable the processes of reflection and review. For beginning teachers, reflection cannot just be examination of curriculum, best methods, and achievement data. Novice teachers need to deal with frustrations, insecurities, and vulnerability. Without attention to these emotional aspects in the teaching profession it is difficult for beginners to develop the special combination of perseverance and passion that some call "grit."

The development of innovative and reflective teachers is paramount for effective schooling. Professional Development requires dealing with conflict, discord, and sometimes bitter and hostile colleagues. Training mentors to deal with the personal <u>and</u> professional challenges of teacher development and empowering them to orchestrate the growth and development of beginning teachers allows interdependence within the ranks of teachers. A professional development program led by trained and empowered mentors would enhance the professionalism of teachers and promote a shared leadership within the school community. However, mentoring programs are often short-term measures, providing initial support and guidance that stops or diminishes early in a teaching career. A culture of mentoring acknowledges the reality that beginning teachers often remain stuck in survival mode and a high percentage of experienced teachers stagnate in their own growth and development after just a few years.

Tony Dungy in his book *The Mentor Leader* (2010) indicated that it's not possible to be an "accidental mentor." Creating a culture of mentoring requires (a) a leader who believes in this and lives it; (b) trained and empowered teachers that are able to practice mentoring constantly, rather than random and infrequent occasions when they are assigned this role, (c) there exists a clearly defined purpose that is the basis for mentoring, and (d) mentors possess a heart for others combined with an understanding of how to enact professional and personal growth.

A culture of mentoring with consistent and focused deliberations not only provides the support and guidance that beginning teachers desperately need but it also builds up the commitment of mentors. Mentors begin to feel valued and galvanized in their work, often renewing their own professional vitality. Working with a novice teacher can be highly rewarding and additionally it keeps the mentor's own teaching fresh. By giving permission to mentors to lead the professional and personal development of new staff members a school's leader creates an opportunity to strengthen leadership within the building. Yet this is rare. Frequently, when teachers return to their own classrooms after learning opportunities, collaborative efforts, or professional development events, something is lost, opportunity to grow has slipped away leaving little or no trace. Developing a culture of mentoring in schools is extremely difficult. There exists a tension between the role of passing on teaching wisdom gained through experience and helping new teachers develop autonomy, creativity, and self-reflection. Mentoring in schools, because of a lack of clarity about goals and purposes and the development of a mentoring disposition, often results in mentoring being little more than helping beginners feel comfortable as they start a new job and providing lesson plans and other resources.

Recently I presented my thoughts and ideas about mentoring at the National Mentoring Institute's National Conference. The room was packed with a combination of teachers and building leaders. Immediately following my presentation, I had the opportunity to have three significant conversations with educators that were present in the conference room. Each conversation contained a similar frustration: how to get building/organization leaders to believe enough in the potential of mentoring to share leadership and empower the mentor. One of the most important lessons I learned as a coach was discovering my influence grew when I allowed my assistant coaches to play a stronger leadership role facilitate my team leaders taking on more of the leadership duties/needs. When I saw them as leaders and helped them become the best leaders they could be, even though in some ways my position diminished, my influence (and our success) grew.

Professional Development programs that are site-based and continuous reveal the highest level of success in teacher growth. School leaders can augment the professional development of beginning teachers by cultivating the leadership abilities of experienced teachers. Enabling potential mentors to create a vision of professional development and granting them permission to implement the necessary systems to make it successful lays a foundation for teacher growth and development to be sustainable and enduring. Creating a culture of mentoring just might be the most influential thing a school leader can do to strengthen commitment. Not only does a culture of mentoring help beginning teachers become effective and help schools with retention but the consistent examination and articulation of teaching strategies helps the mentors continue to grow and develop their own practice. For many teachers, after a few years their improvement stagnates and along with this stagnation, passion wanes. Mentoring a young, passionate beginner helps mentors see the role of teacher through "new" eyes. It allows a veteran teacher to hold onto the ideal that learning is a meaningful endeavor, and they are participating in something that embraces both the past and future success of the school and its students.

On June 12, 2019, I was fortunate to share a two-hour lunch with four beginning teachers of secondary mathematics. All four of these individuals were just finishing their first year or getting ready to start their first year. Early the next day, as I sat with an open journal and reflected on the previous day that I spent with these former students I realized this "event" captured several features of mentoring that can inform and inspire a culture of mentoring. I share the list of ideas *that were clearly present during the conversation or resulted from this simple but thought-provoking experience. First, this was an <u>optional activity</u> that all of us <u>wanted to participate in</u> and it occurred in a <u>different venue</u> than a school building. The agenda was based on the <u>needs and experiences of those in attendance</u> and each person was "allowed" to <u>be an "expert" for a bit</u>, sharing struggles, successes and solutions. While I was the instigator of this gathering, I found myself <u>listening</u> more than leading. The two-hour block of time undoubtedly left its mark on all of us producing and promoting (a) reflection, (b) shared ideas relative to common challenges, (c) affirmation of the reality that some struggles are really dilemmas with no real solution but still problematic, and (d) most importantly future connections.*

I arrived thinking that I would be providing most of the information and inspiration and yet left informed and inspired. One of the ideas discussed was that much of practicum experience for pre-service teachers (of mathematics) comes up short of being impactful because of issues with confidence. These successful new teachers indicated that they themselves battled with weak confidence relative to content, empowerment to interact and lead instruction, and in themselves relative to making connections with kids. Here are the final words of my journal entry from June 13: "This affirms so much of TwE...or at least seems to... in order to make experiences meaningful, the world of inspiration needs to be acknowledged, addressed, and acted upon...for some, this happens naturally but for most it takes an intentional effort to build. The day was so rewarding and served to remind me of something I already know but encountering consistent reminders in the form of memorable moments was very uplifting. I was able to feel enduring because I was reminded that connections are hard (at least if you want them to last) but <u>they are worth it...worth the potential heartache...worth the time..worth the effort.</u> I finished the day drained in a good way. I went to the watch the movie "Rocketman" based on the life of Elton John, who found grand success (based on fame and fortune) but felt so unworthy until he found the ability to be loved...feel loved...let go of shame. I found myself thinking of Keith Browers (a former student-athlete who passed away in 2015) who shared the following quote when I visited with him a few months before he died: "If you laugh, you think, and you cry, that's a full day. That's a heck of a day. You do that, seven days a week, you're going to have something special." – Jim Valvano, National Champion basketball coach and founder the V-foundation

PRINCIPLE 5: WE ARE MORE THAN TEST SCORES

My career as an educator provided me the opportunity to be in many different k-12 classrooms. Often, I witnessed beleaguered teachers (and student teachers). The demands on teachers regularly leaves them drained and discouraged. Pressure to produce evidence of achievement through rationality can leave teachers disheartened and feeling insignificant.

All teachers strive to produce good test scores but without an infusion of inspiration and purpose, mandates and metrics will dampen or destroy meaning. Numbers do not, by themselves, motivate people. It is only when a culture of caring and purpose exists, that drives the desire for good results, can teachers' effort be enhanced.

School cultures that harness wholehearted effort typically include rituals that infuse a spirit of community and inspiration throughout the school year. Rather than one-time events, often intended to gain compliance or buy-in with reform requirements, rituals become part of "who we are" and become anticipated moments. Rituals provide the opportunity to constantly renew the spirit of a teacher and "provide a vital tie to the past, reinvigorate the present, and offer a welcome promissory note to the future" (Deal & Peterson, 2009).

Early in my career I began to understand the power of a ritual. As a coach of endurance runners, I would typically use bus rides home from an "away" competition to discuss what I called the "good and the bad" regarding the just completed race. Then I would award a t-shirt to the "runner-of-the-week." Rather than let a competitive effort go un-analyzed, I used what is often wasted time, with the team messing around or sleeping, to examine, discuss, and reflect. Once I failed to give the "good and the bad" talk and almost immediately the student-athletes begged for those special, heart-felt words. It had become part of who we were to examine our effort together.

Years later, at a different school, one with no traditions and little support for cross county I had to drive the school van to away competitions, with my focus turned to the road, combined with a school culture where many athletes rode home with their parents after athletic events, I lost the opportunity to use the down time to examine and discuss effort with my team. Needless to say, this powerful ritual was never implemented, and I failed to create the kind of culture where endurance runners thrive.

PRINCIPLE 6: WE KNOW WHAT WE STAND FOR

As mentioned earlier, I spent five years completing a Doctorate Degree in education. During this entire stretch of months, I was working full time, either in higher education or as a middle school teacher. In the completion of any advanced degree there is at least one moment of truth where extreme doubt must be overcome. Typically, this comes with a big task that tests one's resolve and endurance. The coursework was mostly a breeze, and I was able to complete the six credits per semester by making my early morning time focused and devoted to this work. I love to learn and the required courses (focused on Teacher Leadership in the classroom, in the school and in the community) allowed me to see things through the lens of my current circumstances and apply them in my roles of teacher/coach/mentor.

Yet, earning this degree nearly broke me because of the dissertation. Over two years of interviewing teachers, analyzing the data, looking for common themes in the growth & development of beginning teachers and then meeting the requirements of my doctoral committee, Institutional Review Board (IRB), University Review Board (URB).... was a highly demanding and draining stretch of months. Oh, how I wanted to quit! There is no doubt that I had to draw on everything within me to keep going. I know that my background as an ultrarunner helped me "stay in the race." I understood that even when things seem hopeless and it feels like you can't take another step, you can pass through a tough stretch and feel good again…that beyond a stretch of miles where you feel worse than you've ever felt before you can recapture that ability and desire to run, even when, at the moment, you can barely walk.

Maybe it's because I consistently encounter young professionals who express the thought, "I feel lost!" that I feel compelled to expand on the idea of knowing what "we stand for". These individuals often are fighting tears as they express doubt in their ability and desire to keep going in their current circumstances. Remember that endurance is more than the ability to bear a hard thing, but to turn it into glory. Too often, when drained physically, mentally or emotionally, it becomes easy to feel defeated. I know when enduring a tough stretch of miles in a test of endurance if the thought of quitting enters your head it is nearly impossible to fully exorcise it and regain a confident, energetic, and enthusiastic drive to the finish line.

As a coach of endurance runners at the high school level I remember telling my athletes "If you're committed to everything then you're committed to nothing." I urged athletes to make sacrifices to narrow their priorities for an upcoming season, knowing that even though they would experience a strong sense of "missing out" on fun this could be replaced with something more significant and memorable.

Similarly, Jim Collins, author of *Good to Great*, said that "if you have more than 3 priorities, you have no priorities." Teachers of impact understand that teaching requires a level of sacrifice. Yet there is a high level of satisfaction in doing something significant and making a difference in the lives of young people. This significance, sometimes called fulfillment, comes from a strong sense of purpose, and being part of a team. Without purpose and community, the sacrifices of a teaching life will wear down or wear out most teachers, at some point in their career.

Keith Brophy, a business leader, and former entrepreneur of the year in the State of Michigan among other honors and accomplishments, shared the thought that a crucial practice for developing a strong team culture in new business ventures includes creating vision, not just in words but in the hearts and minds of each team member. Keith stated that a vision needs to be realistic, understood, owned, fully embraced by the team, and well-rounded. He indicated that it takes courage to do this with fidelity because it is often met with rejection or half-heartedness. As a business leader he intentionally pursues making vision real for his team and has developed two activities to help his team become "vision holders." First, he starts every meeting with a message about vision that reminds the team that "we are more than just a business." A second practice sprang from a vision for new businesses demanding three prongs: <u>respect for all</u>, <u>understand the power of profit</u>, and <u>make the world a better place</u>. Every meeting begins with each team member sharing one thing they had done or experienced that met one of the three components of the organization's vision. Keith indicated that sometimes this practice results in something shared that seems trivial. More often someone shares a powerful story, but always it includes a chance for everyone to contribute to the sense of mission within the organization. Without consistent reminders of vision, it becomes easy for teachers to develop an "it doesn't matter" attitude in words and actions. I believe these business practices shared by Keith can illuminate potential strategies to help all teachers become visionaries and creative contributors to the entire school.

During the last moments before the start of a race I would have my team gather in a "huddle" where I hoped to provide a quick reminder of race goals, race plans and the challenges ahead of them. We would typically end the huddle with something quick, enthusiastic, loud and energizing that helped cement the thought for each of us that "we are ready, and this really matters." There were times when these huddles, that lasted only a minute or two, felt electric, like a current flowing through the team. I know that sense of going to "battle" with one's "brother" or "sister" has stuck with many of the athletes I coached, and I think not only did it produce a focused effort for a group of teenagers but it stuck with them and enabled them to create a sense of energy and focus in other aspects of life.

Roland Barth, author of *Learning by Heart*, indicated the crucial nature of relationships in schools with the following: "As a teacher and then as a principal, I learned over and over again that the relationships among the adults in the schoolhouse has more impact on the quality and character of the school – and on the accomplishments of youngsters – than any other factor." Schools that strive to create strong relationships can overcome the overwhelming challenges that exist in education today. Yet even though the importance of relationships is widely acknowledged, rarely is there meaningful action behind the words. Helping teachers build endurance requires that schools create the opportunity and framework for teachers to build strong relationships with colleagues, leaders, and students.

As a coach I wrote the following when describing how to capture a sense of community within a team of distance runners: One of the most effective ways to build a collective spirit on your team is to demonstrate the belief that everyone's effort matters. Modeling this and expecting it is important in building a fully connected team. I have watched coaches celebrating with their top runners while some of their athletes were still out on the course. I tried to follow our last runner in, cheering just as hard for a last place effort as a winning performance. A highly rewarding experience occurs when the last 100 yards is lined with a team cheering on a teammate whose best effort has them near the back of the pack. This practice makes effort the measuring stick of success and generates meaning and purpose for <u>all</u> those competing, not just the top finishers. One of our team's mantras was: "The race isn't over until the last runner is in."

PRINCIPLE 7: WE WILL DEFINE SUCCESS

"Just because we didn't measure up to some standard of achievement doesn't mean that we don't possess gifts and talents that only we can bring to the world." (Brene Brown in *dare to lead*)

Most beginning teachers enter the profession idealistic, with a strong and sincere mission of making a difference in the lives of their students. All too often, this sense of mission fades, getting replaced by expectations that to a beginning teacher seem unrealistic or confusing and far from the dream that brought them into the profession. The current landscape in education contains measures of success that are:

- – Often controlled by others.
- – Entirely quantitative.
- – Mostly meaningless to students.
- – Used because they are easy to administer.
- – Used more for accountability than to measure future student success.
- – Used because they accurately predict success of similar measures of achievement in the future.

The World Track & Field Championships were held in Eugene, Oregon during the summer of 2022. One of the premier events for this championship was to be the Men's 110-meter high hurdles where the U.S. had a chance to sweep the medals. Grant Holloway was the defending world champion, Devon Allen had the fastest time of the season to date, and Trey Cunningham had won the NCAA title just a month earlier. In track & field it has become a standard practice that the fastest allowed reaction-time is one-tenth of a second (.100 seconds). Any reaction quicker than this results in immediate disqualification. With new technology constantly "enhancing" the sport's equipment, starting blocks are equipped with sensors that measure an athlete's reaction-time to the starting gun. Rules indicate that officials are to use this "data" point to assist them in determining the fairness (or unfairness) of a competitor's start. In the semi-finals, Devon Allen's reaction time was .101 seconds. He reacted within one-thousandth of a second to the allowable standard. In this competition, at the time thought to be his last, (he had signed an NFL contract to play football for the Philadelphia Eagles), within weeks of the death of his father, he seemed poised to win. In the finals, with all three Americans prepared to race well, the gun went off followed immediately by a shrill sound indicating a false start. Technology showed that Devon had reacted to the gun in .099 seconds, one-thousandth of a second faster than the allowable time. Even though the rules state that these sensor-produced reaction times are just one data point in assisting officials, it was the ONLY data point used. Devon was disqualified and his dream of being a world champion was lost. Have we allowed technology and data to rule in a way that, instead of enhancing our lives, they steal moments when we might be better than ever before? In one race, Devon was .001 seconds slower than the suggested reaction-time. In the other, he was .001 seconds faster. One resulted in an opportunity to move to the finals and have a chance for victory and to honor his father. The other led to him walking off the track, defeated before he even raced.

In a profession where success is measured more and more by quantitative measures of achievement, as defined by tests based on standards of content, there exists a risk of loss. Potentially the most tragic loss might be the sense of mission owned by beginning teachers entering the profession. Our profession's measures of success are often far from meaningful to the students in classrooms across our county. This compels beginning teachers to change. This change might come in the form of embracing measures of success that they don't believe in but are forced to adopt and enact. If they remain true to their beliefs barriers go up between themselves and other teachers because they might "do things differently." The result is either a loss of dreams or a loss of connection. Conformity almost always results in a loss of creativity.

Many schools attempt to develop definitions of success that are meaningful and yet the way business is done keeps things fixed on the reality that "test scores rule." Success in life and learning is so much more than the narrow measures found on most tests. Measures of success need to be deep and multi-faceted. For instance, the following is a list of concepts that enhance success and contributes to the lives of teachers and students alike. However, even though this list might be acknowledged as worthy, rarely if ever, do these concepts make their way into an assessment plan:

- Success is making contributions to community.
- Success is instigating interest and enthusiasm.
- Success is the ability to apply curricular ideas outside the classroom.
- Success is when a learning episode leads to a connection with others.

For instance, in the realm of mathematics education, problem-solving is widely acknowledged as the necessary focus of k-12 school mathematics and the most crucial measurement of future success. Yet even though it is the very first standard in the Common Core State Standards of Mathematics (CCSSM), the application of problem-solving in classrooms across the U.S. remains inadequate or in many cases, absent. When asked about this concerning reality teachers often indicate "I don't have time," or a robust attention to problem-solving would require diverging from what "my colleagues are doing."

To unleash the best a teacher has to give we must recognize and support the creativity and idealism that new teachers bring to the profession. This requires schools to regularly examine, discuss, and adjust measures of success and frequently re-create the vision of excellence in classrooms.

As a coach, I developed a tradition, late in my career, to share a vision of what I thought our final race would look like, sound like, and feel like. It was an "attempt to pour my desire for them onto paper and share that with my team" (Kahrs, 2015). The intent was to help them prepare mentally and emotionally for one of the biggest days of their competitive lives. One year I decided I didn't have time to create this heart-felt writing project typically taking me two hours to complete and then 30 minutes of practice time to share with the team. The athletes pleaded for it. I think the veterans on the team realized how valuable it was to revisit our mission and with that refocus our goals and regenerate confidence in reaching those goals.

In order to find consistent success teachers must, not only provide a variety of ways to demonstrate excellence, but also revisit, redefine, and share descriptions that paint a heart-felt and meaningful vision of possibility. When teachers see their mission as creators of memorable moments rather than "coverers" of content and compliant "carry-outers" of someone else's ideas then we will capture the best possible version each teacher has within them.

"Sometimes the biggest victories we experience are not our own. They are victories we share in because we have played a part in someone's [success] by encouraging them and supporting them." (Hall, Run the Mile You're In, 2019)

Early in my time in Higher Education I was working in my office when a former student stopped by to talk. I was unaware that this individual, a student in a 7th-grade class I taught several years earlier, was a student on my campus. This pleasant surprise served to serendipitously re-teach me an important lesson. He told me that he remembered two things about the year he spent in my classroom. First, he said that he remembers the day I let him sleep in class "when I really needed to sleep." As a foster child he was required to work many hours for his foster parents. They worked him hard. He was often exhausted. Secondly, he remembered my practice of catchphrases from the Rocky movies. One of these phrases, a line from Rocky II, when Rocky's coach, Micky, shouts "What's can't, there ain't no can't", in response to Rocky's statement "I can't do that." All of us face "I can't" moments in our lives. The student told me that when the thought of "can't" enters his head, he hears my voice. I felt affirmed that at least one student latched onto this powerful thought that helps him see CAN in the face of CAN'T.

Recently, on a trip to Michigan, I was able to spend a day supporting former student-athletes at the Bayshore Half-marathon in Traverse City, Michigan. Watching these runners, now in their 30's and 40's, push themselves, seeking their best performance on a humid day, over the 13.1-mile distance was uplifting. None of them won the race. Still throughout the race and the remainder of the day I witnessed these former students exhibit a willingness to hurt in search of their best and do it with palpable enthusiasm, love, and a desire to share it with others, including me, their former coach. I got a chance to see and feel a highly meaningful measure of success – helping students find joy and fulfillment in challenging themselves through running. Far from the trophies and quantitative measures of running prowess was this strong, clear evidence of success. Running was something that remains part of their lives because it helps them continue becoming the best possible version of themselves.

"I've learned that people will forget what you said, people will forget what you did, but people will never forget how you made them feel." Maya Angelou [1928 – 2014]

PRINCIPLE 8: WE WILL BE THOUGHTFUL

At one point in the movie *Rocky Balboa*, Rocky says, "It seems the older I get, the more I have to leave behind." The intensity of teaching in k-12 schools, with heightened expectations and increased demands, has mostly left behind thoughtfulness and reflection. It seems that when we are hyper-busy the reptilian part of our brain takes control, leading to survival thinking rather than a thoughtful approach to work. No one can deny that teaching now includes more duties and details than ever, creating an environment of rushing from one requirement to another. Teachers learn to become reluctant, rarely going "all in" with reforms and new ideas because school improvement often comes in the form of mandates or requirements along with extra work.

My last few years as a k-12 classroom teacher included a new school schedule for four consecutive years. Never was this change accompanied with an examination of the previous year's schedule. It seemed that the "silver bullet" of school success resided in how to divvy up the minutes and hours of the school day.

During the interview process for my dissertation about mentoring I consistently asked questions about reflective practices of mentors and mentees. Every single participant indicated they reflected on their work as teachers. However, not a single participant could describe a reflective practice or consistent actions that resulted from their reflection.

It is well-documented that teachers in the U.S. spend much more time with children during the school day than most high-performing countries. This leaves little time and energy for reflective practices. Reflection needs to be more than "simply taking stock of a personal experience or the observed experiences of others." (Make it Stick, p. 223)

Recently, I made an informal presentation for a school that was attempting to build a mentoring culture. I shared many of the ideas expressed within this document. After the presentation a first-year teacher approached me, saying, "Thanks, I needed to hear this. I was just beginning to think that teaching was nothing more than making copies and yelling at kids."

My dissertation (2011) uncovered a connection between culture and reflective practices. It seems that when educators fail to think beyond the technical skills and rational processes their future growth is stunted, even prevented. In a profession that is ever-changing, teachers need to be constantly adapting to new challenges and requirements. Interview data from the dissertation indicated that even veteran teachers placed in the role of mentor are hesitant or reluctant to act without permission or guidance from building administrators.

This reality is particularly damaging to the growth and development of early service teachers. When teachers reflect deeply about issues of belief and purpose, they seem to gain a more fervent confidence in their ability to lead a classroom and make decisions that will positively impact the lives of students. In an un-reflective culture teachers become compliant implementers of someone else's ideas and creativity and growth is lost. With this loss, a sense of purpose is weakened. When purpose is weakened passion fades.

Beginning teachers need assistance in developing a reflective practice that delves deeply into all aspects of teaching. This is mostly uncharted territory. Constant growth and development depend on a consistent and balanced practice of deep reflection relative to, not just skills, rational methods, and organizational competence, but also the human aspects of teaching. When reflection reaches to the core of a teacher, with attention to beliefs and identity, then a sense of mission is consistently nurtured.

In numerous interviews with teachers this inability to access deep and authentic reflection was revealed. Many schools have required teacher meetings, often referred to as PLC's (Professional Learning Communities). Regularly beginning teachers indicated that while these gatherings would sometimes provide support or guidance with technical issues, "there was no way" they would share struggles or doubts. Even more alarming was the consistent finding that mentors would not provide significant and necessary feedback to beginning teachers because they did not feel comfortable "going there" when referring to the tough conversations about individual weaknesses and challenges.

Just like any good habit, reflection needs to be instigated and then practiced. A robust practice of reflection is elusive but can become part of a school's culture. When conversations of depth are valued and become commonplace then it becomes natural and teachers begin to look forward to, rather than dread, opportunities to meet and work together.

PRINCIPLE 9: LEARNING CAN BE FUN

Late in my k-12 teaching career I took a position at a small, rural high school in western Colorado. This decision possessed several components, but I distinctly remember thinking that moving to Colorado allowed me to live a dream of being near the mountains with the opportunity for frequent mountain adventures. With 25 years of teaching behind me, I thought that I could spend the remaining years in my profession "coasting" to retirement, still doing what I was trained to do but investing less in the profession that had left me drained and a bit disillusioned. I justified this intent, thinking that I had given much to the profession for a quarter-century so a little less than a whole-hearted effort would still result in a "pretty good" performance in the classroom.

My new classroom was next to a veteran Language Arts teacher, a few years younger than me, who possessed incredible passion and enthusiasm. I found myself talking with him between classes, at lunch, after school, any time there was a momentary break from the intensity of the teaching day. What I remember most is laughter. Our conversations about the teaching life sparked joy. As we stood outside our classroom doors greeting students on their way to class we often were laughing, and this drew students and other staff into our conversations.

There is no doubt that as our students witnessed the visible joy we shared in teaching many were affected in a positive way. After nearly twenty-five years working incredibly hard I had begun to believe that coasting was an appropriate way to finish a career. Having my joy reignited transformed my perspective. I remember the moment when, instead of feeling drained, I felt energized with the belief that I had more to give…that my experiences and memories created when living the life of a teacher/coach were worth sharing…that coasting was no longer an option. I became inspired to finish my career helping young teachers endure in a profession that can all too often extinguish the wholeheartedness that ignites passion and effort. Rediscovering joy alongside another dedicated teacher made all the difference. That experience helped change my perspective (that quite honestly had weakened). Sometimes a little perspective is all we need to recapture endurance.

The rational world with its propensity to measure and base success solely on achievement data has mostly stolen or at the very least marred the joy within the teaching profession. A classroom with a playful environment that accepts mistakes as an effortful attempt to learn helps build the pleasure of success. There is strong evidence that the recent decrease in play time for children, replaced with more time for math or the language arts, is counterproductive. Similarly, a work environment devoid of a playful atmosphere dampens a joy-filled perspective that relieves tension and brings people together.

Learning and interacting with and about significant ideas and problems can be highly motivating. Yet one only must spend a small amount of time in a high school to witness bored and unengaged students who quickly set aside assigned tasks in favor of social media or idle chatter. I believe that one of education's most important goals should be to help students discover and live out their passions and purposes. While helping our students develop critical skills is part of our profession's role, it is more enduring if we inspire them daily to "wanna know" and "wanna do" their very best. This can only happen in classrooms that are enlivened with a joyful attitude and led by teachers who understand that teaching is much more than covering content with narrow intellectual goals.

For the most part, teachers will determine whether a school will be effective and successful. The U.S. spends a considerable amount on education yet has underinvested in teaching. We continue to spend more and more of our education dollars on management of teachers and measuring of results but neither of these builds the capacity of the very resource that impacts the success of schools the most: teachers. Professional Development efforts need to recognize that teaching never is about "just one best way." Unlocking passion and purpose in students requires passionate and purposeful teachers. The key to building this capacity in teachers is a consistent recapturing of the joy that lies in making a difference.

Recently, I was observing one of my college students as she taught a fifth-grade math lesson. I had several interactions with students but the one that stuck with me was with a student in describing the work her group had accomplished and what was still unfinished said, "Now we get to do the FUN stuff!"

This preservice teacher had embraced the idea that "Math Can Be Fun!" Instead of a focus on answers and procedures to finding the volumes of different rectangular prisms, students constructed rectangular prisms and put them together strategically, creating their own unique "city". When we embrace the belief that learning can be "fun" the classroom becomes a place where academic work turns into "play." There is strong research indicating the importance of play in shaping young brains, fostering empathy, strengthening social interactions, and nurturing creativity. I maintain that consistently including components of "play" in our weekly plans helps us become more than a "coverer of content." It facilitates a mindset and teaching practice of creating memorable moments and memorable is inextricably connected to endurance.

PRINCIPLE 10: WE WILL RECOGNIZE WHAT REALLY MATTERS

Mentioned earlier, I have heard numerous times, from administrators and politicians, the idea that "we will always do what's best for kids." Rarely is that concept the guiding light for educational decision making. What is best for kids is to provide them with teachers that possess a highly developed sense of purpose and a clear perspective of what really matters.

Recently the following priceless gift was posted on Facebook by a former student-athlete of mine: "I know this sounds cliché, but one of the greatest life lessons I learned from Coach Kahrs is that the value you receive from an activity is proportionate to your effort. You might be smart enough to get an A with very little work; however, the value of an education is not measured by one's grade. Pour your heart into what you do and you might fail – but you gain far more value from the activity than the talented person who coasts by on their talent. In education, running, and life – heart is the great equalizer."

The heart of a teacher is fragile. Teaching is demanding and draining and highly personal. Attempts to dehumanize teaching by removing the heart aspect diminishes the profession. Data alone does not motivate people. It's a culture of caring, passionate, and purposeful teachers that drive the numbers.

All teachers enter the profession incomplete. Every beginning teacher needs to learn more and gain meaningful experience. Yet most Professional Development efforts fail to acknowledge the idea that rationality without inspiration does not last; metrics without meaning does not endure; scores without significance do not live on in the hearts and lives of students.

Near the end of my career as a teacher in k-12 schools I was working with a 7th-grade math class that contained many struggling students. One student that was labeled as special needs struggled more than the rest. Even though she regularly attended after-school help sessions she rarely experienced success or even a basic indicator of proficiency in mathematics. One day I gave the class a tangram puzzle problem, intended to have them explore with the tangram pieces in anticipation of using them as a visual for a problem that dealt with ratio & proportion concepts. This young girl who continually "failed" at mathematics was the first person to solve the tangram puzzle. She demonstrated her solution to the class and couldn't hide the smile that came with her "success."

I would like to say that this successful moment led to a future filled with mathematical success. It did not. However, for several years after this memorable moment I would see this young lady (usually at the local Walmart), she had moved to the high school and then to a regional tech center after high school. She would give me a hug and say (with joy), "Remember when I was the first person to solve that puzzle." That moment was memorable for her, and thus it became memorable for me. (I can never forget the look on her face and how her arm shot in the air with the exclamation, "I got it!") I embraced the repeated celebrations of insight with this student who was never going to become a mathematician and yet that one moment helped her see challenges through a lens of "I CAN." It helped her believe, just a little stronger, that she could find solutions to the many "puzzles" of life. The ritual of reliving that moment helped keep that belief alive for years following that tiny success.

A lifetime spent working with teachers convinces me that tiny victories like the one described above happen all the time. Yet these stories are not told often enough. Sharing these kinds of stories helps create a communal bond within a school, carrying messages that illuminate what really matters. A school culture that intentionally roots out these stories and creates a habit of sharing them facilitates personal and professional connections at a deeper level. When educators within schools connect at a level deeper than ordinary and have conversations centered around things that really matter then they build the confidence to stay tethered to their goals and beliefs, respond rather than react in the emotionally charged decision-making within a classroom, and consistently work from a position of self-awareness. Living and working in this kind of environment constantly revives purpose and passion.

The ritual of sharing personal stories and tiny victories is needed more than ever. The landscape in education has become so dominated with processes, mandates, rules, prescriptions, metrics, and the like, that matters of the heart go unacknowledged at best and disparaged at worst. Our students need and deserve the very best education possible, and the quintessential component of a worthy education is a wholehearted teacher. Recognition that wholeheartedness needs constant renewal is a key understanding in creating the kind of school culture that nurtures wholehearted habits and practices.

Early in my career, a highly regarded administrator began a ritual of bringing roses to faculty meetings. Everyone in attendance was given the opportunity to grab a rose and use it to acknowledge the good work of a colleague. I think the rewards of this simple, inexpensive "award system" were immense. Being able to share a story of success about a colleague with the whole staff provided rewards for both the giver and receiver.

WHERE DO WE GO FROM HERE? FINDING THE GLOWSTICKS...

Experience informs me that teaching has become a diminished profession. The hearts and minds of many teachers have become clouded with uncertainty. On the one hand they hear the voices of failure and on the other they hear the demand for change built on reforms and mandates that have little meaning in the lives of the children they work with daily. Many schools have become sterile places with narrow and limited goals. School leaders, in many cases, have taken their "eyes off the ball" and allowed rational solutions to push lifeworld considerations to the bottom of a school's priority list.

In my last few years as a k-12 educator I was always provided with mountains of data to share with parents at Parent Teacher Conferences. I was able to share with parents how their students performed on a variety of assessments, covering many content standards. Consistently, after sharing this information with a parent, they would pause, lean in, and ask, "But how is my child really doing?" These parents recognized that achievement metrics tell only a small part of the story. Test scores measuring responses to what are often easily-measured, skill-based questions mean little in the lives of children. Yet we have allowed these kinds of systems to dominate the work of teachers leading the classrooms where our children spend countless hours.

Teaching with Endurance (TwE) began as a collection of ideas, insights and stories intended to encourage and inspire teachers bogged down in a disheartened state, but I hope for it to become a movement. TwE as a movement has much to overcome. I believe it to be a movement that has a stake in the future of schools within the U.S. Now is the time to reimagine and recapture what truly matters and nourish the things that will endure. What matters most is creating meaningful experiences for our children. What needs nourishing is the lifeworlds of teachers who work with these children. This can only happen with a revolution of sorts. That revolution is a combination of embracing change that makes sense and resurrecting the buoyancy and purpose that inspires teachers to become more than just "coverers" of content, but memorable leaders of instruction that uncover enduring lessons.

TwE is a perspective along with a collection of actions and habits that can help schools find a "sweet spot" of balance between the lifeworld and the systemsworld; between the rational solutions that provide method and structure and matters of the heart that renew passion and purpose. TwE is intended to be a blending of philosophy and support that revives the belief that our children can become powerful thinkers and doers of meaningful things, and the belief that teachers can be creators of classroom environments where children thrive as they begin their own journey of purpose.

TwE is an opportunity and a promise to schools. Schools, perhaps most of all, are organizations that need someone to come beside and help lift the eyes from the "crap" at their feet towards the possibility and potential of the lives of students and teachers alike. The opportunity comes in the form of Professional Development intended to inspire teachers rather than give them strategies with the narrow goal of bumping test scores a bit higher. Wagner

& Dintersmith (2015) in the book *Most Likely to Succeed* stated the following, "If the top priority of our education system were engaging and inspiring kids – not testing and measuring them – all sorts of things would be possible" (p. 251).

TwE could become a reform initiative that focuses on inspiring the very people that will determine whether a school becomes a bastion of hopes and dreams or remains where Wagner & Dintersmith indicated many schools are mired: "a system driven by achievement that is oriented by rules deliberately steering students towards compliantly following a singularly focused pathway. Our world needs graduates that are rule-defining, driven by building relationships, innovative and creative in thought, and polymathic in focus." In many ways TwE is a daring challenge to the current landscape in education and many might think it unworthy in a world that worships at the altar of measurements and systems. Like the connection to the movie *Jerry Maguire* mentioned earlier, I have already felt the sting of ridicule and rejection in sharing my thoughts and experiences from a lifetime in the teaching profession. Still, I see TwE as the instigation of a vision that makes cultivating school culture the truest indicator of success. In a profession where teachers are dead last among all professions in saying their opinions count, TwE wants to provide an enduring reminder that their lives and their work matter.

I recognize the challenge of genuine and enduring change. Much of what is done in school is entrenched in the past and protected by a culture of "this is how we've always done it." Real change cannot happen without the community within a school embracing it on many levels. Nonetheless, there are steps a school can take to begin the journey of undiminishing the work of teachers. The first step includes a compelling message that helps remove barriers. Many aspects of school culture hinder the conception of community and only in building real community can the confines and restrictions of tradition and the status quo be broken down and the true potential of teachers be tapped. For teachers to develop and thrive as wholehearted leaders in the classroom they need the support of a school culture that values change that makes sense. Building this kind of culture is elusive but is the critical aspect of staff development.

In the book, <u>David and Goliath: Underdogs, Misfits and the Art of Battling Giants</u>, Malcolm Gladwell explains how David beat the unbeatable warrior, Goliath. He indicated that in many ways history has it wrong by saying it was purely chance or God's intervention, that delivered the victory to the underdog, David. While I believe that God does intervene on our behalf, I also believe that we can turn the tables on the "giant" of challenge in the teaching profession by seeing things differently. Gladwell alleged that we've been telling the stories of underdogs "wrong" and in many ways it seems to me, we've been telling the stories of teaching success wrong, as well. Late in my career, a veteran teacher said to me, "Kahrs, you're weird. You're a math guy who leads with his heart." Teaching is all about heart. The endurance to sustain the heart of a teacher requires more than just acknowledgement but also actions that help teachers maintain a wholehearted life. Neuroscientist, Antonio Damasio, said "we are feeling machines that think." Building endurance includes a plan to attend to matters of the heart with a high level of fidelity.

The mission of TwE is to provide a compelling message and to facilitate the creation of a vision along with practices that make endurance for teachers a reality. Like the story about getting lost in a dark forest because of missing glowsticks the teaching profession has become lost. Thinking that with systems and procedures, with accountability and increased demands, we can fix education has us wandering off the trail. While we should do some of those things in the systemsworld, I maintain that the most significant answers come from enhancing the lifeworlds of the most important resource in the profession: teachers.

RECOVERING SOME REMINDERS

In the summer of 2017, my never-ending pursuit of challenge and adventure had me in Gould, Colorado for a mountain race. The Never Summer 65-mile ultramarathon was an event that had runners competing over treacherous terrain on trails in the Colorado State Forest, where the average altitude is over 9000 feet. Warnings of potential moose or bear attacks were given frequently. I had competed in longer races and races with challenging, mountainous terrain, but never one that combined high levels of challenge in distance, terrain, and danger. I had the additional challenges of age and was still feeling the effects of a fall earlier in the year that cracked a rib and hampered my training.

I started the race, along with approximately 300 other "crazies" in the pre-dawn hours of July 22, 2017, with a goal of finishing under 23 hours. This would qualify me for the Western States 100 (the granddaddy of trail ultramarathons). I was as prepared as I could be. Months of training, over three weeks of that training at altitude, a runner's backpack filled with stuff to protect me from the elements and provide calories to keep me fueled for the long day ahead.

The most important component of my preparation was enlisting a crew. The intensity of the challenge necessitated having a crew to meet me at different checkpoints and provide support along with a pacer to accompany me in the later stages of the race when fatigue and darkness could lead to increased danger, getting lost, or prematurely dropping out. As I look back, I realize that while I knew having a crew was important, I did not understand just how crucial my crew would be. Nor did I fully understand the rewards that would come my way from sharing the challenge with others.

I finished the race in a little over 21 hours, beating my goal by nearly two hours. For my efforts I received a small chunk of wood with the race logo burned into it; a small memento of a huge physical effort. BUT what I really got was so much more! Three young men traveled far and with great expense to support me in this personal endeavor. The race rules allowed me to have a pacer (someone who runs alongside the competitor) from mile 39 to the finish at mile 65. Each of my crew of three served as a pacer for a portion of that last 26 miles. Each one provided unique and powerful support, guidance and encouragement that helped me overcome nausea, fatigue, and the ability to keep going when night settled, the temperature dropped and navigating the course became difficult. I will never forget those final miles. With my goal well-in-hand I allowed my pace to slow and be comfortable (as comfortable as one can be after spending all day on a mountainous course). I basked a bit. Sharing an incredible adventure over many hours afforded the chance to catch up with my crew on the nearly 30 years of life that had passed since I had served as their coach and teacher.

It has been several years since that day. More of a personal challenge than a race. And still the warm glow of success remains. That small chunk of wood sits on my desk (now a coaster for my morning coffee). I need no physical reminder of that day because my reward was one of human connection. My investment in the lives of three men back in the late 80's and early 90's, when they were teenagers, paid me the most priceless dividend I could have hoped for – a simple reminder of a mantra I've always tried to pass on. This mantra can fade away as the demands and discouragements of life take their toll. The reminder that IT DOES MATTER was renewed as I shuffled those final few miles with all three of my crew by my side. I crossed the finish line at just after 2AM accompanied by Chris, Jeremy, and Eric. It was dark and cold. I was weary in mind and body. I could barely stand but my spirit soared.

MILESTONE MOMENTS (AND ENDURING LESSONS)

When I was a kid, I discovered that I liked to run. It was a discovery that happened slowly. I attended a private Lutheran school, kindergarten through eighth grade. Athletic opportunities were sparse but each spring there was a field day where track & field took center stage for all Lutheran schools in western Michigan. I still have many vivid memories of those days running, jumping, and throwing in what felt like highly competitive events. It seems funny now, but back then (late 60's and early 70's) the 440-yard run, was the grand finale. A race of endurance where all the older kids raced 1 full lap around the track. Being the last event of the day, all the other students along with the parents and fans gathered in the bleachers to watch the best runners from each school battle for the most significant blue ribbon of the day.

I remember watching some of my early heroes (8th-graders when I was in the earlier grades) succeed or fail in this race. I remember having the thought that I wanted to win that race when I got older. I remember watching the fastest kid in our school finish dead last in the event after leading for over half the race. At some level I understood that the race required more than talent. To win this race you had to be fast, but you also needed endurance.

As a 7th-grader I earned the opportunity to represent my school because I was faster than all the 8th-graders. I still remember lining up to run feeling incredible anticipation, but also a degree of fear. I had never performed before such a big crowd in an event where pain was inevitable. I knew it would hurt but prior to this day I had never really pushed through the pain. I still remember a little bit of the pain and the sting of failure (I finished fourth, one place from an award). Fortunately, what I remember most is making a promise to myself that the next year, as an 8th-grader, I was going to win that race.

Brad Kahrs

For the first time I began to build understanding of commitment, training, and sacrifice. Back in the early 70's (just about the time Frank Shorter won the Olympic marathon, instigating the running boom) many people believed that if you trained hard you would use up your allotted energy. I had no access to training advice but what I did have was the experience of becoming a pitcher (baseball and softball) alongside my dad over several years. That experience told me that if you outworked your competitors, it would pay off. I began to run. In the winter I was wearing boots and running through the snow. I ran a mile or so, every day. During the school year I would run my mile right after lunch while my buddies would sit and wait for me to finish so we could play (fortunately for them it would only take me about 6-7 minutes).

By current standards one mile a day is not that much running and my training methods were not specific to the race for which I was preparing. However, I did one thing very well. Something that, at the time, I didn't understand. Even as "just" a 13-year-old boy with a simple dream, without knowledge or a coach, I was developing a habit that would inform my life in a powerful way. What lesson could a young teen-age boy uncover that would continue to provide guidance, even now, over 38 years into a career as an educator?

Every mile logged, every time I ran, each time I laced on my tennis shoes (yes, I wore cheap tennis shoes…remember, this was prior to my knowledge about what might be available and advantageous…it wouldn't be until two years later that I had my first pair of running shoes), I visualized the place, the competitors, what it would feel like as I rounded the last corner and just maybe what it would feel like to win.

Just a year earlier, I had watched my first Olympic race. In 1972 at the Munich games, a young runner named Steve Prefontaine had made headlines with brash predictions and impressive performances. He said that to give anything less than your best was to sacrifice the "gift." Pre believed that each race was a work of art. His words resonated deep within me, and I carried them in my head as I ran the fields and apple orchards near my home. Each row of apple trees was a race where I would picture a rival from another school that had always beat me. He was bigger, stronger, and faster. Each year since 2nd-grade he had outrun, outjumped, and outthrown me. But, I had found a secret. By visualizing my dream and rehearsing it over and over and over again, I was building BELIEF. I was preparing to do something I had never done. I was readying myself to face the pain. Most of this work was done alone. As I look back, I realize that I would have benefitted from training with other runners but there were none.

The race itself was amazing! I will never forget the sense of calm that came after the starter's pistol fired, the drive to the finish after my rival had passed me briefly near the half-way point, seeing my older brother standing near the track where I would be three-fourths of the way done to tell me how far I was ahead (or behind)…I never felt any pain yet I collapsed immediately after crossing the finish line. I had trained to block out all negative thoughts, even physical pain. I even remember a sense of wonder when I found out that I had broken a long-standing field day record (which stood for several more years until my younger brother broke it as a 6th-grader!).

This true story has stuck with me for nearly 50 years. It helps me rekindle the things that slip away a bit easier now that I am over 60 years of age and have a career of more than 39 years. I have no doubt that having a dream, visualizing that dream, and, of course, fulfilling that dream, set the course for a life of rewards. My mission in the time that I have left is to help teachers cling to those hopes and dreams of experiencing memorable moments with young people.

In a profession where we strive so hard to do things right, I believe we should focus on the right things and become masters of those things. There is strong evidence that 4 out of 5 teachers begin their careers with the dream of making a difference in the lives of students. Yet it seems that this is either stolen or at the very least dampened. This loss or weakening of resolve results in only about one in 10 teachers remaining highly passionate and purposeful. Thoreau said, "Most (wo)men live lives of quiet desperation." I sometimes wonder if many teachers are quietly desperate, diminished because a loss of vision, having their dreams of doing significant things trampled by duties and demands.

For several years I worked in a classroom adjacent to a young teacher with a high level of passion. This teacher possessed strong understanding of his subjects (mathematics and physics), but what I remember most was his passion for students. He would greet them daily at the door to his classroom, often saying something like, "Today, we get to play math." Just a few years later I saw discouragement take over the heart of this teacher. No longer was he at his door but in his chair. He still greeted his students in a friendly manner, but the special enthusiasm that provided energy to his lessons and the excitement to learn he passed onto students, had faded.

When dreams of teachers die it becomes difficult to visualize and attain that grand sense of fulfillment that comes when a young person lights up with joy and desire to learn. I still hold onto moments like one early in my teaching career when I had enacted a lesson about solving equations with pre-algebra students that had gone particularly well, ending with an activity, and hearing a student, who had previously expressed a "hatred" towards mathematics, say to his friends on the way out of the classroom, "That was awesome!"

One of the roles in my former job as math educator at University of Wisconsin – Stevens Point was that of student teaching supervisor for secondary mathematics. One spring day, I completed two observations at different junior high schools for two student teachers teaching 8th-grade mathematics. The morning visit included visible energy, joy and discourse as the students worked together on a variety of problems dealing with the topic of the day (Pythagorean Theorem). I witnessed laughter and high fives. The student teacher shared homemade cupcakes as a reward for the students' effort on the previous days' assignment and in the last three minutes of the class period had the students apply proportional reasoning to answer a question about the number of chocolate chips in the entire batch of cupcakes. The second visit started with a negative message about the previous days' quiz scores. The class period was bereft of discourse. Communication was dominated *with complaining from the students and threats from the (student) teacher to gain compliant behavior and get the work done. This visit ended in tears.*

As I drove the 50 miles back to campus, I pondered how two student teachers, both in the same cohort and working with the same age group on the same day, with nearly identical experiences in their academic work, could produce such drastically different results. The answer was simple. One teacher focused on the students, their thinking, their energy, their doing the mathematics. The other focused on the "what" – the completion, the results, the answers. One ended with high fives, the other with tears.

If we are going to help teachers attain AND maintain their dreams and imaginations, we need to help them do the right things. In choosing the "right" things teachers become genuine in the eyes of their students. Students, particularly at the secondary level, will shut a teacher out if they sense they are not authentic. Once that happens the words a teacher says, the lessons provided, the work assigned will make little difference in the lives and learning of the students.

Several years ago, just after leaving k-12 schools and entering the world of higher education I was assigned to teach my first *Secondary Math Methods* course. I learned much during this experience. It is interesting to look back and see clearly how little the university I worked for acknowledged the value of preparing teachers of mathematics. This course, the only Math Education course offered, was a 1-credit course. The first time provides many opportunities to fail, and I failed spectacularly. Some of those mistakes led to important lessons for me and my students.

My first cohort of pre-service secondary teachers included only three students. Each was a unique individual and the "class" possessed diverse backgrounds. One was a traditional student with excellent grades, high enthusiasm and on her way to becoming a successful high school mathematics teacher. The other two were non-traditional students with families, struggling to earn a degree while working full time. One of these non-traditional students was from Japan and had just recently moved to the U.S. because her husband had taken a job in the area. Despite the language barrier, I learned much from this student as she consistently compared U.S. schools to Japanese schools.

One of the lessons that grew out of that experience resulted from a short discussion that poked a bit of fun at the need for acronyms to dominate presentations and conversations in education. One of the students, with a smile on her face, asked, "So Dr. Kahrs, what is your acronym?" The implication, half in jest, was that I needed to develop an acronym to gain notoriety and success. On the spot (one of those rare moments of brilliance or just good luck) I coined the acronym ERPP. Engage, Relationships, Plan, Prepare. I stated that these were the keys to successful teaching for early service teachers. I believed that then and I believe that now. In my work, my research, and my experiences, both as a classroom teacher and as an observer in others' classrooms, I have determined that our profession acknowledges the need for engaging lessons and developing relationships yet beginning teachers receive minimal guidance and support in these areas. Our profession provides instruction in content, along with much guidance in developing structures, and procedures in planning the day-to-day activities in a classroom. However, it is within the realm of the second "P", prepare, that our greatest gains can come. Preparation includes being ready for the discouragement, despair, rejection, disillusionment, dealing with increasing demands often with an "or else" message, disappointment, and indifference that comes from working in the human endeavor of teaching young people. Preparation is all about doing the right things. Doing the right things is the "glowstick" that guides our way to endurance.

BECOMING GENUINE — RIGHT THING #1

It has been my good fortune to have visited many schools in several different states during my career. My work in higher education provided me the opportunity to be in schools nearly every week. Sometimes these visits included classrooms where young students were just beginning their schooling, others high school classes filled with 12th graders ready to graduate, and still others to every grade level in between. This was the best part of my job. I got to witness many "teachable moments." I also witnessed mighty struggles teachers dealt with in order to instigate achievement. The most crucial of these "struggles" is creating an environment where learning thrives, and lessons are durable.

I think that the first step in creating the conditions where durable lessons are common begins within the teacher. Students will only value what is said and done within a classroom if they trust the person leading the classroom. Students believe in those they deem genuine or authentic. Genuine teachers work at building a strong measure of trust with their students. A foundation of trust makes it possible to build high in performance and desire. This sounds simple but is incredibly difficult to create and sustain. It is demanding because it happens little by little and is easily shattered or lost. Yet, when built it can last forever in the hearts and minds of young people. When teachers are seen as genuine by students they become memorable and the lessons they teach become memorable as well.

As a coach I tried to be alongside my team as much as possible during a workout, often running the same workout as them. I saw this as an attempt to share the pain. Even though it was always easier to stand and watch. Even though alongside meant I would have to choose where in the pack I would run. Even though this choice typically narrowed how much and how many athletes I would be able to observe on a given day. Rarely did I miss the opportunity to be alongside my runners during a long run or intense workout.

Additionally, some of the events we competed in would have a "coaches race." Frequently I chose to run in these competitions. Most of these races were held very early in the morning or later in the day when spectator presence was mostly non-existent. Seldomly was there any awards or recognition. Still, I competed and always ran hard. Even at the State Finals I would find a way to share the pain. At most championship races (Regional & State) a small group, usually me, an assistant coach or friend, and a small band of young runners not on the varsity team would arrive very early to set up "camp." We would claim a spot for a small shelter from the weather. While the set up was being finalized, I would "race" the course, usually trying to run at a challenging pace. I wanted to feel what they would feel later in the day.

For all the mistakes and failures, I encountered along the way to becoming a teacher, one thing I did right is believe in and work at building a practice of authenticity. This doesn't just happen! Being seen as genuine can only happen when we are trusted. I believe that young people today experience a loss of trust constantly. They get let down by friends, in many cases parents and siblings, and sometimes teachers. Too many times I have heard a student say, in reference to a teacher, "They just don't care." Now, more than ever, students need to have someone to believe in, trust in.

I advocate three key concepts that help a teacher become genuine in the lives of students. First, I urge you to work hard at developing the quality of empathy. With a strong practice of empathy, we can help young students gain a sense of belonging. When students feel like they belong they might develop an attitude of "I wanna be there" (in your class). Students frequently struggle with the barrier of thinking "it's just me" or "they don't understand." As described above, my coaching practice of "alongside" allowed me to be more empathetic to the challenges a particular course or race conditions posed to a young athlete, still developing the resilience to overcome adversity. Empathy allowed me to listen with the same level of purpose I held when trying to lead a practice or a lesson.

Secondly, though in some ways it may seem counterintuitive, vulnerability is the key that unlocks the door to trust which, in turn, leads to the creation of authenticity. In my undergraduate studies I remember being told, ardently, that I shouldn't smile until Thanksgiving. This admonition always felt misplaced and fed the idea (still existing today) that being the leader in a classroom meant a teacher always must be strong and in control. Sadly, this led many teachers choosing to hide emotion rather than sharing it.

In her book, *dare to lead*, Brene Brown defines vulnerability as "the emotion that we experience during times of uncertainty, risk, and emotional exposure." It is crucial for teachers to harness the power of emotions and vital for them to see vulnerability, not as weakness, but as the cornerstone of trust. When we allow ourselves to be vulnerable enough to share our struggles and mistakes in an open and honest way it helps us be seen and heard as genuine (because we all have struggles and make mistakes). Too often, I have observed a teacher become angry or embarrassed because of a struggle or mistake, instead of modeling vulnerability and helping young people develop empathy and trust-building behaviors.

In 1995, a former student-athlete of mine, was killed in a car accident. Steve was a close family friend and neighbor. He was a hero to many, including my own kids. His death was an incredibly painful event for my team and my family.

It was something felt throughout the school where I worked because Steve was one of those special people that all students saw as accepting. He seemed to easily connect with anybody and everybody. His enthusiasm was unmatched. I remember wrestling with the decision to go to work the Monday immediately following his death. Early in the day, during a Pre-calculus class, I broke down and stepped into my office which was dark and out of sight to my students. As tears streamed down my face, a student walked in looking for help with a math problem. She saw me as the heart-broken human that I was. I had never been particularly close to this serious student, yet in that moment she was permitted to see her normally "in control" math teacher as a hurting individual and it strengthened our connection.

Additionally, I offer four trust-building actions that might help teachers develop an environment of trust in the classroom. Each of these actions became part of who I am. I believe each, if practiced consistently, lead to results that enhance one's endurance. Some of these concepts have been mentioned earlier but I bring them up here within a context and intent of authenticity.

1 – Pay attention and listen. Even though it was mentioned earlier, a focus on listening helps us notice and understand what a student needs to move forward. Rather than a "do it my way" mentality (which blocks a strong listening practice) a teacher who really listens might be heard saying, "that's interesting, tell me more" or "would you be willing to share that with the class?" or "do you think that will work if…"

2 – Ask for help. Recall the "Max Burns" story from Principle 3 in an earlier chapter. I have found great success in asking for help from students IF the tasks I ask for help with are significant. As a coach, after a home meet, it was required to pick up and put away all the markers used to guide runners over the 5,000-meter course. Early in my career I would be out there alone for up to two hours taking care of the equipment. I decided to ask for help. Helping coach with this task eventually became a privilege and when the school purchased a John Deere "gator" everyone wanted to help with the menial task of clean-up (because they got to drive the gator).

3 – Gestures of genuine care and connection. Something small but heart-felt can make a huge difference. A note or card with a specific, individualized message is something that can last forever. Something as simple as an "atomic fireball" because a student needed a lift can bring a smile to a young person's face.

4 – Use assessment to provide "I believe" messages. There is no doubt that students benefit from messages that express belief in their efforts. Writing these on the back of key assessments or stapling a belief message to the back of a student paper is a powerful practice. I worked hard to only provide these with challenging tasks AND look for opportunities to give these strategically to all students during a given semester.

As a math teacher for many years, I came to believe that mental math (the ability to compute without pencil & paper or the use of a calculator) was one of the most important, life-enhancing skills I could promote and develop in the classroom.

A mental math practice I developed over time was to meet students at the door and hand them something. Typically, this "something" was a small piece of paper that students understood was supposed to be turned into a mental math answer sheet. Students knew that on the back they were to write the numbers 1 to 10 along the left-hand side of the paper as answer slots in preparation for mental math which would begin at the bell. Always there were 10 questions which made determining percentages easier. There were many positive results from this classroom practice. It provided an active and engaging start to the class where students had to focus and listen. The mental math activities I utilized allowed me to review and preview certain mathematical ideas. As a math activity it provided a robust opportunity for students to share their thinking as they visualized a method required in an estimation or calculation. I maintain mental math helps students "see" mathematics as a visual subject. I loved hearing one of my students say, "Oh, now I see it!" Students grappled with the belief that there is just one way to get an answer and learned the valuable lesson while there always many ways, sometimes there exist better ways. I remember hearing many positive reactions to a student who completed the problem using an interesting or unique strategy. Perhaps the most memorable aspect of mental math in my classroom was the enthusiasm and props I used to promote mental math as a worthwhile activity. For years I used a jellybean dispenser, given to me by a student, (that I nicknamed JB) to provide a tiny bit of motivation for mental math. JB was a red, jellybean-shaped dispenser that when the right button was pushed would drop a jellybean out into one hand, toss it over his head through a clear plastic tube, where it landed in his other hand and a student could claim their prize. I recognize in this new COVID world this would no longer be appropriate, but I think the value of JB was more than the tiny candy prize. As students would enter the room, JB was sitting on my desk often prompting a smile or an exclamation about the impending mental math, and throughout the activity I would talk with gusto about the ever-present smile on JB's face because he got to participate with his favorite thing, mental math.

I think becoming genuine in students' lives and learning is enriched when teachers employ a uniqueness to their classroom practices. My mental math practice allowed me to pour out a special brand of joy and further a playful atmosphere in my classroom. Was it effective? Maybe. Was it memorable? Definitely. Journalist and author, Adela Rogers St. Johns said, "Joy is a light that fills you with hope and faith and love." Even now, just thinking about all those JB moments in my past, brings a smile to my face.

Over 30 years ago I coached a team that included a very memorable collection of female athletes. One of the athletes on the team (mentioned earlier) consistently brought a high level of enthusiasm and persistence to practice and competitions. Even though she would usually finish in last place, she never let this deter her from showing up and working hard the next time out. On a Monday afternoon in early October "Jen" had her day. I had competed in a 50-mile race just two days prior and showed up for practice feeling the effects of that effort. Still, I was committed to the practice of "alongside" my team. On this fall day the team headed out to a sandy powerline for the planned workout. We used 1.5 miles of "easy" running on a gravel road as a warmup. I was struggling. I couldn't keep up. Down the gravel road and throughout the workout over the sandy hills of the powerline I was the last runner. At the end of the workout, I spoke of how much it hurt to just put one foot in front of the other. I shared the difficulty of doing a workout on sandy hills that make each uphill step a monumental effort. Facetiously, I asked the question, "who would create such a tortuous workout?" I will never forget the moment at the end-of-year banquet when Jen shared her memories of the day "she beat coach." It would have been easier for me to beg off and not run that day, but I would have missed a grand opportunity to be alongside my team on my toughest of days. I hurt a lot that day. I had vulnerability thrust on me. I will never forget the words and the hug from Jen that served to mark a memory for me and her. This enduring lesson means even more now as old age and wear-and-tear have ravaged my body, often placing me in the back of the pack.

CREATE A FAMILY — RIGHT THING #2

One of my treasured themes that I worked diligently to create in every class I taught or every team I coached is that of belonging. As a teacher of Advanced Placement Calculus back in the 1990's, a student who was a senior at the time, said to me, "You know what I like about this class? We are like a family in here." Several years later while teaching in another state and working with 7th-graders labeled as "below grade level" I heard the same thing from a student. Early in my work as a university professor I heard it again from an adult student. Each of the classes mentioned here achieved success beyond reasonable expectations. I look back and understand more clearly that the success was mostly the result of an environment of belonging.

I have been an endurance runner for over 45 years now. I have logged many miles, likely over 90,000 miles, which has created some "wear and tear" on my body. What I know for sure is that some running surfaces are hard and unforgiving, some are very soft and sap my strength, but there are some running surfaces that have just the right amount of "bounce" and seem to propel me forward, helping me want to run farther and faster. As an educator, I know a teacher can capture that "bounce" when the classroom environment includes a sense of "family." It is important for teachers and teacher leaders to acknowledge and help develop strategies to build practices that promote an environment of "we are in this together." This "bounce" not only helps students want to invest effort but also provides teachers with that little extra desire to do everything possible for these students. The "bounce" helps students and teachers care a little bit more, dig a little bit deeper, thus propelling them forward towards a bright future.

I have mentioned the "family" theme several times in job interviews. I have since thought more about the importance of creating close-knittedness within the classroom. Doing the right things cannot be practiced outside an environment that values human connection.

One of the things I realized late in my coaching career was that my most successful teams shared a consistent habit which can be applied to teaching and learning. It was the habit of "lingering." I look back now, many years later, and understand the important role that lingering played in the development of my athletes. After a tough run or a race, they wanted to be together and talk about the challenge, conditions, pain, or what was next. These talks were filled with laughter or tears, sometimes anger or disappointment, sometimes hope but always talks filled with love and depth. It seems that the habit of lingering adds meaning and purpose to the endeavor of distance running. I suspect the practice of lingering does the same for the teaching and learning process. Lingering allows a practice of reflection to take root and with it capture the significance of strong effort.

Similarly, a great memory in my teaching career is related to the habit of lingering. During a school year where I had developed the habit of eating lunch in my classroom to catch up on my work of grading or lesson preparation and steal a few quiet moments. This plan quickly slipped away when a couple of students asked if they could eat lunch in my room. I agreed reluctantly, not wanting to lose those stolen minutes in a hectic school day, but it ended up making an immense difference in my days. That lunch period quickly became the hi-lite of my day. More and more students began bringing their lunch and eating in my classroom. I suspect part of it was to avoid the noise and craziness of the cafeteria, but I think it had more to do with the intimacy of a lunch period with a small group of people who wanted to be together. Sometimes there were discussions about struggles in certain classes, sometimes challenges with other people; always there was an openness, hard to capture in typical school settings. What I remember the most is the amount of laughter. We laughed often and heartily. We reveled in being together. The students who came to Kahrs' room during lunch that school year <u>wanted to be there</u>. *It was their choice to linger. Sadly, that was lost the following year when it was mandated that all students eat lunch in the cafeteria with the instigation of a monitor at the cafeteria's exit to make sure this was happening.*

DEVELOP YOUR OWN GOOD PRACTICES — RIGHT THING #3

Late in my career as a k-12 teacher I participated in a Professional Development event for beginning teachers and their district-assigned mentors. I was there in the role of mentor and the participants had just separated into small discussion groups defined by subject area. Each small group contained beginning teachers (required to be there), some of the mentors (not required to be there) and one randomly assigned administrator that was supposed to lead the discussion. Early in the discussion, which was mostly focused on issues the beginning teachers were struggling with, my mentee shared her biggest challenge. The pre-algebra class that she taught during the last period of the day was particularly unmotivated, poorly behaved and difficult to engage in the learning of mathematics. She spoke of how hard she had been trying to get these students to participate and contribute to a positive learning environment. This novice teacher expressed a strong sense of failure and frustration. Without asking a single question the administrator declared a solution: "Just differentiate." On the ride home the beginning teacher shared infuriation with the administrator's response. Without listening to the vast array of strategies she had already employed and a description of the support this novice teacher had sought and received this administrator saw the solution through a narrow "best practice lens." I remember feeling exasperated with this seemingly simple solution. After the sharing of an extreme challenge with a high level of vulnerability from a novice teacher the "expert" indicated that classroom success could be found by just adding an additional layer of differentiation.

I believe there are many teaching practices that are effective. What bothers me is the idea that there exists a special list of best practices that when implemented correctly will solve the challenges faced by classroom teachers. How we communicate ideas of effective teaching practices impacts the growth and development of beginning teachers in powerful ways. Parker Palmer, author of *Courage to Teach*, said that "there are no formulas for good teaching and the advice of experts has but marginal utility." As the above vignette reveals, our profession often tells beginning teachers that there is a very specific list of things that they should be doing and if done "right" they will not experience the challenges that are vexing to them. This can be discouraging to a beginner because they might struggle to understand or implement a particular "best" practice. Furthermore, telling a young teacher to "just do this" steals the opportunity for a novice teacher to be creative in overcoming the challenges that can be perplexing. I am not suggesting that instruction of "best practices" should be removed from the growth and development for teachers, but I do believe that how this instruction is shared proves crucial for beginning teachers.

As a coach, I was constantly searching for and reading about training plans for successful teams and individual elite athletes. Similarly, as a teacher, I felt I learned much in observing or talking with a teacher about upcoming lessons and how they would be enacted. Yet, beginning teachers often receive instruction about teaching strategies that include, directly or indirectly, the message that "you should do this AND you should do it this way!" Marzano and Lang-Raad (2019) in their book, *The New Art and Science of Teaching*, address the reality that even when using the exact same instructional strategies, two successful teachers "will have shaped and adapted those strategies to adhere to their specific personalities, the subject matter they teach, and their students' unique needs." In other words, "we can never articulate effective teaching as a set of strategies that all teachers must execute in precisely the same way." (p. 1)

Developing a perspective on what strategies lead to effective teaching is an essential part of teacher development. I offer the following short list of ideas that rather than serving as directives of "best practices" I hope serves as guideposts in a teacher's individual development of their own good practices helping them find success and fulfillment through the enactment of lessons in a learning environment that reflects their creativity and uniqueness.

Good teaching practice 1: The first five minutes matters. As often as possible plan the first five minutes to engage students in thinking about interesting and relevant concepts within the subject area (or not). An interesting question often activates what I have always referred to as the "I WANNA" in students. When students wonder about something they are nudged to be creative, reflective, deep, and confident thinkers.

As a coach, I recognized how crucial the first few minutes of a race could be for a young distance runner. Often the race is lost because of the anxiety-driven decisions, reactions, and loss of focus that plague young runners. Knowing that the last seconds before the start of the race were challenging for athletes to control their nerves, I would consistently share the words, "you can't win the race in the first few minutes" along with the admonition "be smart early in the race, be tough late in the race." Similarly, the first few minutes of a class session can cause a lesson to be lost, particularly at the secondary level. Still, I have rarely seen the first five minutes of a secondary lesson be utilized to launch a lesson with engaging ideas and actions. I firmly believe that a powerful and enduring professional development strategy in mathematics would be to practice with veracity how to use the first 5 minutes of a class in a way that gains a high level of "I WANNA."

Good teaching practice 2: Let go! It is hard for teachers to let go and allow students to struggle. Yet it is through struggle that students capture durable learning and develop the mindset that challenging lessons can be mastered. As a math educator I noticed that mathematics teaching is too often showing students how (sometimes referred to as a scaffolding approach of I DO, WE DO, YOU DO) and this comes up short of helping students become mathematical thinkers. Mathematics is about reasoning, thinking, exploring, and justifying and not just following directions. Teaching can become "just telling" in the minds and practices of many classroom teachers. Letting go does not let teachers off the hook, they must anticipate student difficulties and facilitate persistence. This is incredibly difficult work. Helping students access persistence and connect the relationship between learning and effort drives students far beyond any lesson of content.

In race preparation I found that there are some things that when controlled by a consistent "process" helped athletes relax and maintain a high level of focus. We called this "keeping our eye on the ball." One of these processes for my teams was the what's and how's of our warmup. There was a very procedural method to our warmup, mostly based on the science of preparing the body for rigorous exercise but also addressing the reality that a team made up of teen-agers is easily distracted. However, the race itself was a more complex event and this is where I tried to promote creativity in the way an athlete approached race strategy. Steve Prefontaine (Pre), one of the most famous distance runners of all time, is credited with the belief "A race is a work of art." As a coach I tried to "let go" with the decision-making during a race. I suspect that early in my career this may have hampered some runners' performances. Ultimately, though, it provided a sense of ownership that helped athletes view their role in training and racing in a more meaningful way. Likewise, in the classroom there are some things that should be driven by procedures, but many times teachers need to "let go."

I consider a teachers' perspective and practice of dealing with mistakes and "failure" to be perhaps the most fertile ground of all for passing on enduring lessons. I know this to be true in mathematics education where work in many classrooms is "answer-focused" rather than "idea-focused." Students discern whether they can arrive at correct answers quickly and often shut down, unwilling to risk their ideas and solutions because they are judged "right" or "wrong." Keith Brophy, a business leader and entrepreneur mentioned earlier, indicated that in the business world it is crucial that employees learn to "fail fast" and move on from inevitable failure in the ever-changing world of developing new businesses. In education if we pass on to our students the mindset that failure is a grand opportunity to learn, not something to be avoided, we prepare them for a life of overcoming setbacks and moving forward to success.

Malcolm Gladwell writes about the idea that some difficulties are desirable, even though most people would think otherwise. He captures story after story of someone with a huge personal challenge yet through the process of overcoming the challenge becomes better, stronger, wiser. I think instruction and practice focused on dealing with student mistakes, that includes the seemingly trivial notion of what language might be used to address mistakes, struggles, and difficulties provides teachers with both the perspective and the tools to help students see classroom work as much more than arriving with correct answers. There is no doubt when classroom conversations focus on thinking and ideas as opposed to "what did you get?" students develop an ability to converse with complex ideas without the burden of judgement holding them back.

Good teaching practice 3: Together Everyone Achieves More. I once was asked a question about learning that has stuck with me for decades. That question was, "if you can't explain it effectively to another person, have you really learned it?" Good instruction includes consistent and frequent opportunities for students to share ideas, explain their work, and justify their solutions. I believe that one of the most important contributions of k-12 schooling should be development of the ability to communicate complex ideas in a way that helps another understand. This rarely happens in isolation. When a classroom becomes team-oriented not only can the learning of content become deeper but the opportunity to teach lessons of respect, empathy, cooperation, collaboration, listening, risk & courage, trust & vulnerability, acceptance, and a sense of together that promotes helping others.

When teaching and learning includes frequent and robust opportunities to discuss, explain, and justify, students take ownership of their learning and responsibility for their understanding. Some experts refer to this as *metacognition,* and in many classrooms, this is a dramatic change from a common practice of the teacher providing all the ideas and given requirements to students. When the teacher controls all the thinking and how a task is approached, a very narrow definition and application of learning is employed.

As a coach I wanted to help athletes take ownership of their training. I felt like my greatest opportunity to instigate this crucial but often ignored aspect of training was during the summer months. While it was against state rules to hold mandatory practices in the summer it was critical that athletes build a base of miles that allowed them to train hard once regular practices began in mid-August. Informing and inspiring them to log these summer miles was a big part of the success of teams I coached. Not only did this get the athletes fit and avoid injuries but I think it steeled them by fueling determination. They developed a powerful two-fold perspective with the investment of time and effort during their summer months. First, they held the individual thought that "there is no way I won't succeed after doing all this hard work!" Secondly, they realized how much easier it is to train with others and collectively they began making connections of encouragement and accountability with teammates.

Good teaching practice 4: Make assessment about WE not ME. Assessment is a grand opportunity to build community and help students believe that they have something worthy to contribute to the greater good. However, when the focus is on grades and individual achievement this opportunity is lost.

My first year in Higher Education provided the opportunity to spend a lot of time in one second-grade teacher's classroom. The leader of this classroom was a Master Teacher. Her math lessons were engaging and required students to explore, create, share, discuss, explain, and justify. Students had fun and it seemed evident they saw math more as playing than working. The reality was that they were encountering difficult concepts and building deep understanding. However, in late January of a school year where I was a frequent observer, things changed. Suddenly math time was individual practice with worksheet after worksheet. I can look back now and understand what happened. But for one 2nd-grade boy the change was confusing and one day he raised his hand and asked, "Ms. Smith, are we ever going to do normal math again?"

The second grader, mentioned above, at his young age, revealed that too often the things that we do in the name of helping students achieve is not what helps them learn in meaningful ways. When we make assessment seamless and part of how "business is done" in the classroom, where student ideas are the "currency" then students will see that their thinking and effort matter. When assessment includes not just attempts to produce right answers to exercises that might prepare students to perform better on achievement tests but also opportunities to examine and reflect on how they learned mutual responsibility is enhanced. As mentioned earlier I call this the "200% rule" (based on Bruce Wilkinson's *Law of the Learner)*. When teachers believe that they are 100% responsible for the learning that will take place but continue to inspire the belief in their students that they are 100% responsible for the learning that will take place powerful lessons are learned. When we access 200% then the teaching and learning process is powerful and meaningful. Without 200% it is often frustrating and discouraging. Assessment and how we apply it in the classroom is at the heart of the 200% rule and the process of metacognition, helping students achieve a crucial goal of becoming effective lifelong learners.

Good teaching practice 5: Look through the lens of inspiration first. This is something that I have applied all my life, but only rarely have I been successful in passing this practice forward to other educators. Typically, time is the barrier mentioned as to why this "can't" happen. However, I think it is more about belief. When a teacher holds an undiminished perspective on the role of a teacher then issues of perseverance, caring, determination, acceptance, community, reflection, and gratitude, among many others, become a part of planning a memorable lesson.

I think it important to note that many teachers already apply some or all of the strategies described above. However, it is imperative that these strategies are shared and discussed. One of the findings I uncovered when writing my dissertation is that many excellent teachers rarely, if ever, articulate the things they do that produce meaningful and enduring lessons. This ultimately results in a lost opportunity for a school because it is this awareness and ability to discuss important classroom practices that comprise critical professional development for the long haul and a culture of mentoring that was discussed earlier.

I WILL CONTRIBUTE TO MY TEAM – RIGHT THING #4

There exists research that supports the notion that the power of academic teams is mostly untapped. Having spent most of my life as part of one or more teams each academic year for 5 decades, many of those years in the role of leader, I can attest to both the potential of teams and the extreme challenge and frequent frustration that comes when attempting to build teams. I know that when the team connection is strong in a school, teachers' commitment, resolve, and passion is stronger. Team connections have proven to help with teacher attrition and motivation. Nevertheless, for all the ways that teams can enhance the performance of schools and the lives of teachers, rarely do strong and authentic team connections exist. Throughout the previous pages, concepts of team and a culture of together have echoed through the words, however as our time together draws to a close, I want to reinforce the crucial nature of team in the work and personal lives of teachers. In a list of the right things to do in schools, this might be the one with the most long-lasting impact.

I have been fortunate in many ways. I have experienced the best of team experiences and quite possible the worst. It is my hope that this book fully reveals my effort to provide a meaningful and memorable document for teachers and school leaders. I have attempted to capture important ideas about teams that provide some encouragement in the constant pursuit of understanding and practice of building strong and authentic teams. Throughout your reading you have encountered an array of ideas and practices regarding the together component of school culture, so I feel it appropriate to "tie a bow" on these ideas with some final thoughts about teams because it is true that Together Everyone Achieves More.

As mentioned earlier, my coaching career included the experience of having several of the teams I coached achieve a close-knittedness that while raising the performance of all and producing a strong sense of unity instigated resentment in others outside the team. Several detractors coined the phrase "cross country cult" to level criticism at our team. While the term cult has grown to include a highly negative connotation, the basis of the word is simply a way of describing a group of people that care deeply about something or someone. Sadly, the word was leveled negatively towards my team, and bumper stickers were created by the most mean-spirited of the criticizers in an attempt to hurt the team. While some noticed our closeness and saw it as positive and even inspirational, the negativity of several and the envy they held built a barrier between our team and others, between me and other coaches. One coach saw the closeness and wanted it for her team. She requested the opportunity for her team to attend camp with us (a basketball team going to a cross country camp seemed ludicrous at the time). Perhaps her team's week with a bunch of endurance runners left basketball skills under-polished, but it seemed clear that individual will was strengthened, and the team connection was deepened. I watched in wonder as her team completed one of my team's big challenges of the week, The Dune Run, a 4-mile challenge from a parking lot near Glen Lake over the dunes to Lake Michigan and back. This challenge often breaks the will of seasoned distance runners. Still, her team of basketball players all finished, immediately embracing as a group, many in tears for overcoming something they never thought they could do. I suspect this remains memorable for many; I know it does for most of the runners that went to camp with my team. Even the owners of a motel that served as hosts for our state meet lodging for several years noticed the intimate connection of our team and placed the following quote on the marquee in front of the motel: "Big Rapids Cross Country – A team that beats with one heart."

I think there are many reasons calling for a relentless pursuit of a strong team component within all schools. The three lenses of a teacher's world, <u>cognitive</u>, <u>method</u>, and <u>human or inspirational</u>, reveal why team concerns are so crucial for our profession. First, the waves of change and reform are constant and often confusing. Frequently when these waves recede there exists a message of "You are not enough and need to do more." Reflecting on the reforms of the past and preparing for the constant march of reforms ahead requires a degree of intimacy where frustration, confusion, discouragement, and a desire to give up can be safely expressed. Understanding of education reforms goes far beyond the cognitive realm. Without the opportunity to gain understanding in both the cognitive component of constant reforms, as well as the strategic realm of how it impacts the lives and learning of staff and students, the beginnings of bitterness or resignation take root.

Coaching teenagers provides many challenges and frustrations. One of the challenges is providing a variety of settings to complete the longer training runs. Keeping things fresh and interesting helps overcome the tedium of logging the long miles necessary for building physical endurance. This effort of finding new places to run required running on roads and trails that were initially unfamiliar to everyone. Instigating a team rule of "no one runs alone" was difficult because often teenagers struggle to understand that WE is more important than ME. I would assign groups with the expectation that they stay together but often the result was some getting left behind and alone in unfamiliar surroundings. It was impossible for me to keep track of all runners all the time when they would be stretched out over several miles of trail or road. Overcoming selfishness was a challenge. Many athletes struggled to set aside the thought that "this is my run and slowing down for a teammate robs me of a strong workout." Eventually most athletes grew to understand that the small individual gains of fitness that were sacrificed by keeping small groups together, paled in comparison to the team gains captured with a strong component of WE instead of ME.

The transformation of "me-centered" teenagers into "we-centered" teammates was something I pursued diligently. A vital perspective of team is rarely built solely through a process. It is typically a transformation and in the hearts of teachers it allows them to set aside a "just leave me alone and let me teach" perspective and embrace a "together is better" life. I always felt that the lesson of sacrifice was the most crucial lesson a group of teenagers needed to learn before they became a team. I suspect this applies to a group of teachers as well. Fully embracing a life of team requires moving beyond simple compliance to building strong bonds of trust, which allow effort, commitment, and caring to flourish.

Robert Kennedy has been credited with saying, "There are those who look at things the way they are and ask why…I dream of things that never were and ask why not." This powerful statement indicates dreams and aspirations can be ignited with a concerted effort to understand. This kind of understanding in schools rarely happens in isolation. Seeking understanding and the desire to maintain a wholehearted and sincere effort takes a team effort. It is essential that the potential of team gets unleashed. This is what I've spent a lifetime reading about, thinking about, writing about, and living for. When I find it in strong measure my life is more meaningful. When it is absent, I feel empty. Getting to the point of genuine team includes a setting aside of selfishness, which exists in most of us. This is rare and especially challenging at the secondary level where the daily schedule and differing subject matter erects barriers between colleagues.

WHAT WAITS AT YOUR FINISH LINE?

So why isn't a philosophy and practice of building endurance for teachers applied in a more consistent and intentional way? Many acknowledge the importance of the human components of the teaching world, but it is rare to see strong evidence of this being a priority. The simplest answer is – **it's hard**! It is much easier to do things the way "everybody" else is doing them. Mostly this easier way means seeing the role of teacher as provider of information and strategies to get right answers and demonstrate achievement. It is just plain easier to focus solely on the rational world. A good education needs to balance mind and soul, head, and heart. Like the world of coaching, if all we must do is develop physical fitness the job is much easier than preparing someone to race well over the course of several months or several years, staying motivated and committed to the training it takes to be competitive and perform at one's optimum level.

When taking on the challenge of an ultramarathon I am often asked, "Why?". I know that most endurance runners try to keep that question from entering their heads. I find my most difficult days as a teacher are those moments when the question of why enters my conscious thoughts and I feel at a loss for an answer. As a coach I knew that the last moments together as a team can create lasting memories and additionally help lay a solid foundation for the following season. I used to say that the championships of next year are won on the last day of this season. As we approach the finish line in this writing project, I aim to capture some words that will stick with you, allowing the ideas and actions of endurance to take root in your work and life.

Recently, I got a letter from a former student who later became a colleague. She has left the teaching profession. In the letter, she shared the following thought, "Teaching was possibly the worst profession that I could have chosen." The weight of feeling like she had to be everything to everyone had broken her after more than 20 years in the profession. It is discouraging to know she looks back on her teaching career with heartache and regret. This seemingly successful teacher left the profession with a broken heart. She found it impossible to turn the hard work of teaching into glory.

As a teacher I tried to create memorable moments and lessons that last. As mentioned earlier I tried to orchestrate the final day with my teams to be one that commemorated a season of memories and meaning. As we approach the finish line of this book together, I offer several stories of teachers with endurance, individuals who have touched my life and contributed much to our profession by enhancing the lives and learning of hundreds of students. These individuals provide me with some powerful "why's" relative to teaching being the best of professions because of the consistent opportunities to make a difference. During the hard, dark, uphill miles in an ultramarathon, things are easier if the reasons you run are solid and branded on your soul. Similarly, a teaching career is easier if the reasons you teach are part of who you are. The following individuals and their stories provide me with strong reasons to keep going. They help me look back at nearly 40 years as a teacher with a sense of joy and meaning.

Doug Veysey - Oregon. I met Doug in 1983. He was part of the interview team for my first teaching job at a small high school in central Oregon. He left an impression on me and helped me decide to accept the position despite it being 2300 miles from home and seemingly in the middle of nowhere. His energy and enthusiasm, combined with an obvious love of the school, students and fellow teachers was powerful. I remember thinking, "I want to be a part of that!" There were many reasons why it didn't make sense to accept the job offer but Doug gave me a strong reason why it did make sense and I have no regrets.

Doug is a red-haired Canadian (now more gray than red) who completed his undergraduate studies at Eastern Washington University in 1980. One year later he landed at a small high school in central Oregon where I was destined to meet him in 1983. I sometimes wonder if it truly was destiny that guided my decision to search for a job in Oregon as I prepared to graduate from Grand Valley State University in Allendale, Michigan, travel over 2000 miles to interview, and ultimately choose to move my young wife and two-year old son, across the country, despite other job offers that paid more and kept me closer to family and friends. I have no doubt that if I had not met Doug, as part of the interview process, I would not have accepted the position (and likely stayed safe and close to home). I must disclose that this first job, at a small, rural high school, included the challenge of teaching a wide-array of different classes (6 different preps), but it provided the opportunity to learn some lessons that might only have been learned in such an environment.

This small school (approximately 120 students in grades 9-12), seemingly far from civilization, allowed me to learn lessons that have endured through the years. These lessons likely would never have taken root if I had stayed safe. The first years of teaching are always highly demanding, yet this first job, with its remote location and deep-seated culture that included strong sense of collegiality, helped me forge clear convictions of what I would stand for as an educator. What sticks with me from these two challenging and memorable years helped define a perspective of teacher development that helps me continue to serve teachers with sincere and purposeful effort. I can look back and see this experience as a priceless gift given to me by my life-long friend and fellow teacher, Doug Veysey.

I was fortunate to have my classroom right next to Doug's. As a business teacher, his teaching load included several sections of typing. I was able to observe him greet his students with such enthusiasm that it appeared they were entering a classroom that would be nothing, but a fun-filled 50 minutes spent producing words on a page. Even though I witnessed some students roll their eyes when hearing Mr. Veysey spout his joyful pronouncements, those eye-rolling students were usually smiling. Those five minutes between classes, in the hallway with Doug, had a profound impact on my own teaching. Because I was a first-year teacher my assignment was comprised mostly of "low-level" math classes that included many students who at best struggled and at worst were defiant because they hated math. There were many class sessions that were challenging, filled with failure, and sapped my enthusiasm to teach. Being in the hallway with Doug for 5 minutes of every hour proved to be a regular "breath of fresh air", enabling me to access the precious and much-needed moments as intervals of inspiration. I learned that passion wanes but can be restored. I learned that the best professional development is often close by and when it comes from a trusted colleague it develops strong roots.

There is an even more powerful reason that I include Doug Veysey in my list of teachers with endurance. You see, Doug retired from his paid teaching position in 2012. He has transformed into an entrepreneur and owns a coffee shop in Myrtle Point, Oregon. He approaches this work with the same exuberance that he did teaching. In 2016 I was able to share this part of his new life when I flew out for a visit. He took his coffee shop on the road to a Farmer's Market. I remember thinking that spending a day serving coffee to customers at a market sounded dreadful. Instead, I thoroughly enjoyed the day. It was 8 hours of conversation and laughter. Listening to the banter between Doug and the other vendors brought a smile to my face and reminded me that every day we have an opportunity to impact lives, we just need to "show up." Doug is someone who always shows up with an "all out" approach. Perhaps this is the most important lesson of endurance for teachers. Being able to face the grind of day-to-day details and requirements and continually find, share, and express joy is where the fruits of endurance become real. Even the simple transaction of selling a cup of coffee provides the opportunity to make a difference, sometimes for just a moment, sometimes for a day, and sometimes for a lifetime.

Despite his full-time endeavor with coffee sales, Doug continues to coach and referee throughout the year. He continues to find great joy in being a volunteer coach of cross country and track & field. He consistently finds opportunities to run alongside a young athlete providing encouragement or simply pushing them to be a little better and finish ahead of that 63-year-old coach with a loud mouth. I suspect there have been many who have benefited from Doug's side-by-side energetic rants. He will be remembered. He has a legacy that endures.

Jennifer Magner – Colorado. I was fortunate to work with Jen for a few years as I made the transition from teaching high school students to teaching middle school students late in my career. Team planning at our middle school was based on grade level and we both taught 7th graders, so we were on the same team. We also served together as mentors of beginning teachers and a few years later collaborated with a mentoring plan she was leading as she began her new career as an administrator.

Jen was small in stature (5 feet tall) but she was a powerful figure in the classroom. She started her college career at Colorado State University as a pre-med major. Jen quickly discovered that she "passed out at the sight of blood." This led to a transfer to a small Christian college in Nebraska where she "figured out how to help people even if she couldn't sew them back together." Her love of teaching was uncovered and eventually led her home to Delta, Colorado where she taught middle school science for 10 years. Ms. Magner could be tough. I remember her "marches" through the hallways of our school. If students did not follow proper protocols during a lab, she would march them up and down the halls like a drill sergeant in order to help them learn how to follow directions. I remember seeing her pass by my room in her lab coat shouting orders to her 7th-graders, and the memory still brings a smile to my face.

Beyond the tough persona and high expectations there was a teacher who practiced joy. I am forever grateful that this joy touched my life. Jen's joyful approach to teaching and living was on display for all of us to see and share (sometimes with undesirable consequences). Our school day began outside in the front of the school with announcements and the Pledge of Allegiance. In this western Colorado town snow was a rare event. One rare snowy morning after the pledge she convinced me that creating a snow angel was a good way to start the day. Together we made snow angels in front of everyone, laughing and smiling as we plopped into the snow. I'm sure some of my students thought to themselves, "what's that old man doing playing in the snow?" For the rest of the day, I carried a smile with me, despite the wet clothes I wore, receiving many comments about "wetting my pants." I believe that when students observe teachers "having fun" and connecting on the job it provides a model of how they can work and live with joy.

She combined this daily practice of joy with a determined spirit. Our team meetings during those years were often positive experiences because we, collectively, tried to do what's best for students. Rather than just talk about systems and schedules and procedures we pushed for growth and change, in ourselves, our school, and our students.

I will be honest, over the years as many of my colleagues leave teaching to become administrators, I battle disappointment. I even use the phrase "going to the dark side" to describe this professional change. Many choose this professional change in order to make more money because we all know that teacher salaries are pretty flat, especially in mid-career when most people are starting families, wanting nice homes, and preparing to support their kids' futures. So, when Jen chose to become an administrator, I wrestled with disappointment. Yet her choice, while a positive in the financial realm, came with a sincere desire to use her position to help teachers. In her first year as an assistant principal, she instigated mentoring activities intended to support both experienced teachers serving as mentors along with beginning teachers who need genuine, consistent help and guidance. I was able to participate in these professional development events that were executed solely on the energy and enthusiasm of Jen. Often after these gatherings, where I got a chance to share a few ideas, I remember having significant conversations with beginning teachers and their assigned mentors. As they were learning from me, I was learning with them.

Jen constantly enhances the "why" we teach and understands fully that when the "why" is strong and at the forefront of what we do then capturing joy is much easier. I asked her about her own "why" in a recent phone conversation and she shared a story about a 5th-grade boy that touched her heart. Soon after becoming Principal at an elementary school (grades k-5) she encountered a boy whom she described as "smart, quiet, kind, and well-spoken." This boy, typically "stoic" and reserved, rarely showed any emotion and yet as he sat in the front row of the "continuation" ceremony (he was one of four teacher-chosen speakers) tears were rolling down his face. Jen noticed and went over to make sure that he wanted to continue and give his speech. She thought he was nervous and possibly wanted to back out of this challenging commitment. The boy answered with a determined response, "I want to do this!" The speech ended up being all about Jen. Apparently, this young boy was able to capture in words how one person with a smile and "always being there" made a huge difference in his young life. He recognized how important this was and therefore was compelled to share his story in front of his school about the significance of one difference-maker.

As Jen shared this story with me, she choked up. The emotion of this memory endures. I suspect this is a moment that will remain with Jen (and the boy) forever. It seems to me that teachers with endurance cling to these moments because they provide a way back to the passion that often fades. These poignant stories need to be shared because the simple act of articulating them delivers clear reminders of what matters to the teller and the one hearing the story. These kinds of conversations provide an opportunity to reach out to those who delivered the moment with a message of gratitude.

Erin Stoffel – Wisconsin. As an athlete I trained hard and pushed myself in the pursuit of great performances. As a teacher and coach, I try to instill the pursuit of greatness in the students and athletes I work with. Yet sometimes greatness finds us. Such was the case when Erin Stoffel walked into my office on the campus of the University of Wisconsin – Stevens Point (UWSP). I had just landed in what I intended to be my final professional stop. It was October of my first year at UWSP (2014) when I heard a knock on my door and opened it to a determined, passionate, and intense woman. Little did I know that when I opened the door, I was meeting someone that would change the course of my career.

Erin is a graduate of UWSP, who began her college career as a music major and eventually graduated with a dual major in music and mathematics. She came to my office that day to confront injustice in the mathematics education program our university provided for pre-service teachers. This injustice came in the form of a colleague who was jaded, burned out, angry, and unapproachable. I had already witnessed some actions from this colleague that were, at best questionable, and, at worst, mean-spirited. Erin demanded that something be done about a situation that was filled with complacency and resulted in a failure to support and attract future teachers. I will never forget the intensity of her stare that came with the expectation that I "do something."

At this point in my life, I had garnered experience with just enough wisdom to know that changing the attitude, habits, and effort of my colleague would be difficult, if not impossible. It would have been easy to let the voice of "It doesn't matter!" help me justify doing nothing. After all this was "his" problem, not mine. Instead, Erin's intense demand to "DO SOMETHING!" helped instigate a strong effort to create powerful practicum experiences which resulted in meaningful connections between university students and practicing teachers.

I would like to tell you that my effort impacted the negative colleague in a way that transformed him. I had hoped that with hard work and reaching out to share evidence of success with stories from field experiences, I could instigate change within my Math Ed colleague and the culture within the department. In that I was disappointed. Yet, Erin's courage in approaching a university professor, whom she did not know, to demand justice, provided a platform for creating robust field experiences. Many of my students have benefitted from spending time with Erin. Erin's demand was not just an observation, she offered to be part of the solution. She intuitively understood that our profession needs a rescue, and that rescue must come from within. Erin has opened the door of her classroom to future teachers and this open door includes more than just the opportunity to observe a master teacher. Erin's open door always includes a willingness to have a meaningful conversation.

Erin is one of my teaching "heroes" because when you spend time in Erin's classroom you can witness a teacher who finds a way to build relationships while holding high expectations for all students. She consistently demonstrates a belief that all students can learn and contribute to small group or whole group discussions and problem solving. Erin pushes all students to go deep with mathematical content. In a subject that is typically "answer-focused" her expectation is that students will demonstrate deep understanding with the ability to share and articulate that understanding. Every day I get to spend in Erin's classroom is another day where my belief that mathematics teaching and learning is so much more than covering curriculum is strengthened. Erin's work reminds me of how significant the life of a teacher can be. I count myself fortunate that my final "miles" of a long career were alongside several educators who define what it means to teach with endurance in such a profound way.

Carrie Kunkle – Michigan. Carrie was a student of mine back in the late 80's. I still remember the first time I saw her compete and the first time I met her face-to-face. Her accomplishments as an athlete placed her in "rare air" in our rural community. The list of accomplishments included an individual state title in Track & Field and being rated as one of the best basketball players in the entire state of Michigan during her senior year. She was given a full-ride scholarship to play D1 basketball at Central Michigan University. Yet it was the dignity, kindness and humility that she poured into the people she encountered that I remember most. Carrie attended the school where I taught mathematics and coached two sports for only her senior year. The school she had attended for the three previous years cut all sports because of financial difficulties. Her family "moved mountains" to provide the opportunity for her to continue her athletic career.

I remember being highly impressed with how she handled herself in a challenging situation as she became the "new girl" who was "stealing" playing time from a highly competitive basketball team. As a student she quietly went about pursuing connections with her classmates and teachers along with understanding of course content. As an athlete she pursued excellence but always in a way that invited and included others to share the journey.

In the nearly three decades since I worked with Carrie as a student-athlete she has served as teacher and coach for several school districts. Along the way she has been mentored and served as mentor, developing professional relationships with teachers based on content area and a reality that the role of mentor can play a significant role in the professional growth and development of teachers. It has been incredibly rewarding to see an educator who measures her worth by what she can give (rather than what she gets). Her spirit of gratitude for the daily opportunities our profession provides is inspiring.

I close this vignette of Carrie with her own words:

We have all heard the comment that teachers wear many different hats in education. That is very true. I see this as a wonderful opportunity to observe, listen, encourage, discipline, mentor and demonstrate empathy for our students. We don't always have to provide an answer, but it is so important for students to feel that they are being heard and acknowledged. There are times where it is very painful to see what our students are struggling with and it hurts to watch them grow and sometimes make the wrong decision but hopefully, we can guide them and support them through some of those struggles. That is what teaching is all about.

I love being a teacher and am grateful that I get to work every day with young people. It is tremendously rewarding but it is also a lot of hard work. If I had it to do all over again, even with the ups and downs, I wouldn't hesitate. We have built a living legacy. You are building your legacy one student at a time. Sometimes, years later, we are even lucky enough to have former students who become great friends that last for a lifetime.

As a young or new teacher there are many challenges. Not only are you responsible for preparing your lessons that are aligned to the state curriculum, but you also are encouraged to be a part of different committees and there is always a shortage of volunteers to help with clubs, sports, and extra-curricular events. My advice would be to prioritize and focus your energy on connecting with your students. Building a trusting but assertive relationship will help with so many other components of teaching. When students respect and feel a connection with their teacher, things like discipline, classroom management and general organization and planning fall into place.

So many teachers, over the years, have allowed me to draw inspiration from them and challenged me to continue tirelessly to make a difference in the lives of students. Carrie has endured great heartache and rejection. She has fought all the battles faced by teachers and consistently turned discouragement and disappointment into hope and opportunity. Carrie is not a hero because she purposefully sets out to become a hero, it just comes naturally to her. It is part of who she is and one gets to see it, hear it, and feel it when in her presence or in a conversation with her. I always look forward to the next time I get to see her or talk to her, and I know that will last forever.

Jennifer Bowling – Wisconsin. In the fall of 2008, I traveled to Steamboat Springs, Colorado with my good friend Keith Brophy to compete in a 50-mile endurance race. Steamboat Springs is home to several ski-resorts and the mountains and trails in that area are beautiful. I was living in Colorado at the time and had spent much of the summer hiking and running at high altitudes. Keith had traveled from Michigan and was not very fit. With no opportunity to get Keith acclimated (the race is run with an average altitude of approximately 10,000 feet) we held no aspirations beyond finishing the race. Given 15 hours to cover the 50-mile distance, we looked at the race as an opportunity to spend an entire day together, doing what we loved to do – run. The day was spectacular! We stayed side-by-side the entire time, near the back of the pack, basking in the beauty, sharing the adventure and challenge. We laughed for many of the miles, struggling later in the race as the altitude and miles began to take their toll.

I will never forget the last few miles of this race. We hit the last aid station (about 46 miles into the race) as the sun was setting. I felt like we were glowing, inside and out, from a day spent sharing an adventure surrounded by beauty and reminiscing about more than 30 years of friendship and running. A sunset over the mountains after nearly 14 hours spent pushing yourself to keep going had us feeling satisfied with the sense that "it doesn't get much better than this." The finish line felt close, easily within our grasp as we headed down the mountain. Only four, mostly downhill, miles with over an hour to cover them. We had it made, or so we thought. Suddenly it got dark. We had not prepared to run in the dark and since most runners would finish before daylight disappeared the race management did not use glow sticks to light the trail. We found ourselves on hands and knees trying to find the turns and trail markers that were nearly invisible in the dark forested surroundings. Our hour of "buffer" to make the cut-off of 15 hours quickly disintegrated and we began to feel anxious about making it to the finish line at all. We stumbled along, often sensing a wave of doubt whether we were going the right way. And then, a moment I will never forget!

We popped out of the trees onto a service road and behind us there was a light so bright that despite the silence I thought there must be a huge vehicle with its "brights" on bearing down on us. I turned to see the source of the light and was awestruck with a full moon that had remained hidden from us because of the trees and mountains all around. Suddenly we could see the trail again. The trail markers that had seemed hidden from us became clear. We were laughing again as our pace picked up and we regained the confidence that we were going the right way. Soon we heard the voices and noise of the finish line and made it with 10 minutes to spare. The effort, shared with a life-long friend, combined with the "bright-light" experience made the day a memory emblazoned forever in my mind and on my heart.

In my professional life I had a "bright light" experience in 2017. My work as a university math educator allowed me to visit many classrooms across central Wisconsin. I love interacting with teachers, both in-service and preservice. I understand the challenges of leading mathematics instruction. I frequently get the opportunity to encourage teachers and be present when significant lessons can be illuminated for novice teachers. One large, local high school had just opened its doors to students in a secondary math methods course that I was teaching. My students were required to complete 40 hours of practicum work. For years, this practicum requirement received little oversight and support, included minimal accountability, and most often resulted in university students sitting in the back of the room "observing" classroom activities while working on homework for their other college classes. I worked hard to transform practicum experiences in mathematics education from a mostly meaningless completion of hours into a challenging and reflective component that pushes students to fully instigate the process of becoming a teacher who can lead, inspire and care for students.

Change is difficult, particularly at the university level. Transforming practicum requirements from an item to be checked off a list into a memorable experience was fraught with doubt and discouragement…at least it was for me. I found myself "at the mercy" of classroom teachers who were often reluctant or unwilling to host one or more of my students in their classrooms. Many of those who did host a student modeled little more than the technical skills of covering topics and measuring achievement with ordinary assessment instruments. And then one day I entered the classroom of Jennifer Bowling. Several of my students had contacted me, letting me know they were observing her on a day when I was available. In my attempt to initiate reflection on classroom observations I tried to share as many of these observation hours as possible and then prompt a conversation about the observed lesson.

I will never forget those first moments in Jennifer's (JB) classroom. Her "light" of enthusiasm and energy shined brightly. It was obvious that students were responding and engaging to the "beacon" that stood before and alongside them. JB used her presence in a powerful way, moving quickly from small group to small group, constantly noticing and providing just what a student needed. There was a bounce in her step and a joy in her work that set her apart. JB's ability to ignite smiles and effort was remarkable. She found a way to get to the "right" level with each student which allowed her to make the student feel special and safe enough to share thoughts and ideas. Eventually, I noticed that JB's light extended beyond her classroom walls. I have always believed that classroom leadership, especially at the secondary level, begins before the bell. It is increasingly rare to see this practice implemented. JB does this naturally and consistently. Her exuberant spirit "leaks out" into the hallway, providing "light" to all who pass, even those students not in her classes. Kindness and care are the first things her students encounter as they enter the classroom.

Over the next three years several student teachers and practicum students mentioned that it's a bit "intimidating to work with Ms. Bowling." She is always highly prepared, and that preparation extends weeks, even months into the future. Who does this? Who can keep up? It seems that this hyper-productivity pays huge dividends. Highly prepared translates into JB's ability and willingness to be fully present when a colleague or student is in need. When most teachers are racing to complete the little details that dominate a school day, JB already has it done (usually weeks in advance), which allows her to notice and address the needs of others. As an instructional leader for a large high school, she is constantly called into meetings and "asked" to provide PD activities that are one hour to full day in length. Somehow, she finds the endurance to see these additional demands as opportunities to shape lives.

Never have I encountered a teacher who possesses more on her "plate" but also the ability to see over the heaps of duties and demands. JB frequently turns hectic into helping and busyness into influence. The only way she can do this is with a large component of sacrifice. Her days habitually begin at 4AM. Before her first student walks into her classroom, she has often logged a half-day of intense work. Once the first school bell rings the day often races ahead like a train at full speed. Teachers are often unable to react quickly if something unforeseen is on the "tracks." JB has forged the practice of being prepared for the "debris" on the tracks of a teacher's life by getting up and getting after it before most people have rolled out of bed.

Many individuals are not willing to give at this level and yet those who encounter Jennifer Bowling find someone who turns this sacrifice into something quietly glorious. She has a richness in her life that is inspiring to see and hear. It has been my privilege to hear her own students stop by her room to "just talk", telling her of school or life events. It has enhanced my work and perspective to sit with her and one of my students as we collectively reflect on a lesson taught, examining what can be learned from a teaching episode.

The movie Rocky IV contains an intimate moment with Rocky and his young son as Rocky prepares to leave for Russia to face his toughest opponent ever. The son asks Rocky if he is scared. Rocky's reply is worth hearing. He says, "sometimes I do get scared, and I wish I would get hit so I don't feel anymore but then another side comes out and wants to take more, wants to go that one more round, because going one more round when you don't think you can makes all the difference in your life." Teachers with endurance constantly find the ability to "go one more round" and give of themselves above and beyond what most are willing to give. It has been an honor to work with teachers who live a "one more round" life. The results are amazing and last forever.

Recently I shared the following message on Facebook during Teacher Appreciation Week 2022:

The teaching profession and all those teachers in my circle of friends were on my heart Saturday morning as I headed out for an early morning run in the Wasatch Mountains. I intentionally started before sunrise because I love to watch the sun hit the Oquirrh Mountain range to the west before slowly making its way into the canyons and over the peaks to the east. I knew I needed some of the beauty and warmth that the sun could provide as I started up the trail near the base of Mt. Olympus in 30-degree temps. I was weary from finishing another semester in my 39-year career as an educator. I have seen and felt the intense challenges the past two years have placed on my profession. COVID has taken a toll.

The trail I chose [only minutes from my house] included lots of steep climbing and rocky footing that kept my pace slow, but the route also provided some incredible views of the snow-capped mountains. Sometimes when I head out on a trail, I bring a camera so I can capture the beauty I so often encounter. On this run I didn't and OH, HOW I WISH I HAD!

The mountain stream rushing down Mt. Olympus was like music to my soul. When I broke out of the trees and found the view of the mountains to the south with just a glimmer of light on their snowy peaks, it created a picture that begged to be taken. Still, it was the view I was blessed with about 6 miles into my "run" that I wanted to share with my friends as a metaphor for the teaching life. After about 90 minutes of arduous climbing and rocky footing that kept trying to trip me up and bring me down, I rounded a bend and ahead of me was a stretch of trail with no rocks and lined with the new growth of spring flowers. For about a quarter mile I had smooth sailing. It was glorious! Just what I needed after a long climb. It only lasted a few minutes, but this old, mostly broken-down runner treasured those minutes where I felt a wonderful sense of being (dare I say it) fast.

I couldn't help but wonder if this isn't a powerful metaphor for those teachers who work so hard to make a difference. Sometimes it can feel all uphill with the "rocks" of duty, demands, disrespect and discouragement constantly trying to bring one down. BUT then the "magic" comes, and the "trail" becomes smooth, and it feels "right." I know when a teacher receives a reminder that their work is meaningful it makes a difference for them. Yet sometimes there can be a lot of rocky, uphill miles before you find those memorable moments.

On a Thursday evening two weeks before the end of the spring semester, I was teaching a graduate course, when on a break I received a highly negative message from my program director regarding the weak attendance and insubstantial commitment from a group of undergrads I have worked with over the course of two semesters. Feeling a bit deflated I returned to the evening class a couple of minutes early. Only one student was in the room. This student approached me, thanking me for the work we had shared over the course of semester and handed me a gift. This gift was a book titled "Big Magic" by Elizabeth Gilbert, but the real gift was a note tucked inside that I found later that evening and it brought tears to my eyes. The simple, short, priceless note said, "Thank you for reminding me of the magic of teaching."

If you are a teacher in need of some encouragement, I offer the hope of some smooth and beautiful stretches of trail in the days ahead. These will come. They will likely be in the form of a young person's words or actions or just simply a look that reminds you that YOU ARE A DIFFERENCE-MAKER! [Note: As I was writing this, I received a text message and picture from a former student, now a teacher, about a memorable moment we shared four years ago.]

A TRIBUTE TO MY TEACHER OF ENDURANCE: MARY LOUISE "BIF" (HOWARD) KAHRS [1937 – 2019]

So many times, throughout my life, my mom would say the words, "keep on, keeping on" when I shared a setback or struggle with her. Sometimes, as a youngster I would get frustrated, even angry, and I would wonder, "What does that even mean?" I finally understand what she was trying to teach me. The book you hold in your hands, which began as a personal journal of ideas and experiences that I thought crucial in the development of teachers, has gradually grown into this small book. Several times I set it aside and nearly lost it. Discouragement, disappointment, disillusionment and doubt constantly nip at the heels of educators who lead with the heart. So many times, those "d" words mentioned above felt like a dark cloud of despair. The summer of 2019 saw me approach the finish line of this project, then my mom suffered a massive stroke on September 7 and died on September 12, 2019. This left a huge hole in my heart that remains.

In the days leading up to my Mom's Memorial Service I spent many hours alone trying to understand why my healthy mother, the one who nurtured matters of the heart and soul in me, the one who constantly provided a beacon of love and encouragement, was taken just minutes before a family celebration. Several times over those days between her death and the funeral I uncovered a card or a note from my mom that I had kept, most of them included the mantra, "keep on, keeping on." The deep emotion of losing a loved one helps sear memories and lessons that endure. The lesson that I have pursued for a lifetime and tried to capture in this book is how to embrace these words from my mom that will forever echo in my mind, heart, and soul: KEEP ON, KEEPING ON.

One of my first, intense mountain races was a 50-mile trail race in Virginia that was described as "50 of the toughest miles in the east." The first time I ran the race (nearly 40 years ago) I was humbled and learned one of my most important running lessons. About 35 miles into the race near Massanutten Mountain, I got lost. I went off course for about a mile, eventually finding my way back and to an aid station. I was discouraged and drained after more than 6 hours on the rocky, mountainous trail. I felt defeated knowing that I had just added an hour or more to my finishing time. The Race Director, who happened to be at the aid station, told me that it was unlikely I could make the final cut-off time a few miles later (about mile 40). After all, he had been unable to run that 5-mile section in a recent training run at the pace I would need to stay in the race. The words "NO WAY YOU CAN DO IT" echoed in my mind and I quickly made the decision to drop out and catch a ride to the finish line area. As I was leaving the aid station in a jeep, an older guy trotted into the aid station, heard the same NO WAY message, grabbed a drink and kept going. He was older than me, slower afoot, and had less time to make the cut-off than I would have had. I dropped out. He kept going and finished the race. I watched him finish to applause of respect, admiration, and accomplishment. I learned two lessons that day. As a runner I learned to never make a hasty decision to stop. As a person and life-long educator, I learned to never let the words of someone who is not even in the "race" bring me down.

The intent of this book is to provide a vision like the finish line of a long, arduous race when despite pain and fatigue a runner finds the ability to run with joy and gratitude. For me this is where teaching and running long races intersect. When embarking on an ultramarathon I know there will be some painful miles, sometimes I will be trudging uphill, in the dark and the finish line will seem far off, even unattainable. An ultramarathon can often leave me completely spent, barely able to put one foot in front of the other. In races of endurance, you can get lost, become drained, and feel defeated. In teaching you will hear words from those in the "cheap seats" that will pierce your heart and make you wonder why you do it. You have to get lost sometimes, then make your way back to the reasons why it's worth it.

One of my personal habits is an attempt to block out those negative discouraging voices that steal my passion. I begin nearly every day in pursuit of inspiration. Sometimes this pursuit takes me into the realm of TED talk presentations on *YouTube*. This platform provides new and exciting ideas or inspiring stories, but like the real world of education it also includes voices of dissent for the way we do things. It is my hope that this small book which is a work of "heart" (not a work of art) be seen, read, and applied not as a dissenting voice but as a vision or reminder of how the worlds of systems (data, processes, management) and matters of the heart can coexist, even thrive, IF. I hope to have provided many of the IF's.

Too often, teachers become embroiled in the world of systems and lose track of the purposeful approach to teaching that provides meaning, joy, and the determination to lead a significant life. Nietzsche said, "Genius is a question of endurance." As I begin a personal "sabbatical", I see clearly that endurance is crucial in the teaching profession. Making a difference in the lives of students, for the long haul is a question of endurance and endurance is a matter of heart and soul, needing to be replenished, developed, and consistently transformed or recaptured.

The role of teacher, in my mind, needs to include a component of spirituality. I use this word not necessarily in a religious context but to indicate that to develop endurance and be a "difference maker" for the long haul one needs to attend to the human components of teaching. This means attending to the spirit of a teacher. When the role of teacher becomes a part of who you are so that you ooze it, share it, express it, and instill it, the result is that you become centered and balanced because you know who you are and what you stand for. Inspiration can only be sustained when it is sought, cultivated, and shared nearly every day. I have been fortunate to have continually found inspiration in the work of teaching alongside other teachers. I am grateful that I am consistently inspired by the words of students as they realize their lives have been forever impacted by the work and care of a teacher.

I need to share a story that continues to remind me of the eternal nature of our profession. It starts with a description of a scene I found on *YouTube* from a movie that intersected powerfully with an experience that I had with a student back in the early 90's. The movie, *Coach Carter,* includes a touching scene where a basketball coach, played by Samuel L. Jackson, decides to quit because his goal of transforming the lives of his players is undermined by administration and parents. He believes that preparing his players for the future is the most important thing while other stakeholders seem to think that winning basketball games is what matters most. As the coach is leaving the gym carrying a box of personal possessions from his office, he encounters his team sitting and studying. The group of misfits had come together as a team, committed to finish what they had started. They had come to believe in

Coach Carter's message that becoming your best means more than the scoreboard. This message of discipline, character, and sacrifice was hard for them to embrace but they had begun to see and feel the effects of a transformed heart. The coach's belief that each of them could go to college and have a better life had taken hold and brought them together. Even when given the option of an easier road, without expectations and accountability, they realized that ease is the greatest threat of progress. As the coach begins to turn, seemingly to take his stuff back to his office, the most troubled player, one that almost quit to peddle drugs on the street, stands and shares the following words:

Our deepest fear is not that we are inadequate. Our deepest fear is that we are powerful beyond measure. It is our light, not our darkness, that most frightens us. Your playing small does not serve the world. There is nothing enlightened about shrinking so other people won't feel insecure around you. We were all meant to shine as children do. It's not just in some of us, it's in everyone. As as we let our own light shine, we unconsciously give other people permission to do the same, as we are liberated from our own fear. Our presence automatically liberates others. Sir, I just want to say, Thank you. You saved my life.

This movie scene intersects slightly but powerfully with my life. Over 30 years ago, as a teacher and coach at a high school in Michigan, I discovered that a student-athlete had been kicked out of his home by an abusive, angry father. This young man was intelligent and had helped his team win the school's first-ever state championship. During the winter months of his senior year, he threw a party at his parents' home on a Saturday night when they were gone. His father uncovered evidence of the party and demanded his son produce the names of all who attended. The son refused and ended up on the street. For several days he slept on the couches of friends and acquaintances, but eventually found himself sleeping in the dugout of the school's baseball field. A teammate informed me of this situation, and I immediately brought this abandoned young man into my home and began an attempt to reconcile the rift between him and his father. My wife and I had two young children, a small house, and very little to share besides a place to sleep and food to eat. He quickly became part of our family. The Christmas he stayed with us is one of the most memorable holidays for me, my wife, and my two oldest children.

I worked to mend the relationship between the student and his father. Eventually the student-athlete went home. His homelife remained rocky and difficult but he was able to reconnect with his siblings and remained close to them. The piece of the story I want to share here, as I write the final words of this book, is that for over 20 years, this young man called me, always between Thanksgiving and Christmas, to check in. He always ended each yearly conversation with the following, "Thanks for saving my life."

I share a bit of serendipity that came my way as I wrestled with the homestretch of this writing project. This past winter a book "fell into my lap." That book, *Greenlights* by Matthew McConaughey, gave voice to many of the things that constantly unsettle my heart. For his project, he took a lifetime collection of journals into the desert and pieced them together into a book. Exactly what I've been doing for over eight years, trying to piece the journals, lived experiences, and beliefs about the teaching profession into a document that helps teachers rekindle or renew the portions of their hearts that give rise to passionate and purposeful teaching.

Early in the book, McConaughey writes, "I needed to go someplace where the noise of the world fades and I can hear myself again. As the noise decreases the signals [we need] become clearer. We can hear ourselves and we reunite. Time alone simplifies the heart." As I near the completion of this project I am alone in the mountains of Colorado writing these words in a journal. On this retreat, time has slowed down and those voices of doubt and unworthiness in my head have been (mostly) replaced with a sense of gratitude in my heart. As I gaze up at the surrounding mountains gratitude has washed over me for how the teaching profession and so many individuals within it have enriched my life.

I must share one of the stories from Greenlights that resonated powerfully with me and parallels what I hoped to convey on the pages of this book. McConaughey's book tells the story where he "escaped" to a monastery in a remote area of New Mexico. He went for a long walk in the desert with Brother Christian. As he walked with Brother Christian, he "unloaded my feelings of guilt, the low and lecherous places that my mind had been traveling, the perverseness of my thoughts." Near the end of the walk, Matthew McConaughey was weeping. He had poured out all the stuff that weighed him down. He sat in silence, waiting for judgment. Nothing came but stillness. Finally, he looked up and into the eyes of Brother Christian who had not said a word the whole time. Brother Christian looked Matthew in the eyes "and in almost a whisper, said, 'Me too.'"

I am not proposing that teachers bring the homeless into their homes or escape into the desert (although for some this might prove uplifting), but I know that there are many hurting kids in classrooms across the country and when teachers keep their hearts "alive" and continue to notice, acknowledge, and encourage students through good times and bad times, they just might be shaping, even saving, a life. I urge you to keep going, even when you don't think you can. If you are a teacher reading this and feeling the pain of rejection or the discouragement that comes with a voice of "It Doesn't Matter!" or wrestling with the doubt of feeling like you can't go on or the sadness that accompanies the realization that your passion has faded, I say "Me too." I have been in all of those places, many times, and I am ready to share a walk or talk with you. I provide my contact information for you at the end of this book. My promise to you is that if you are lost you can find your way back to the teacher you want to be. Passion and purpose can be recaptured. A life of endurance is a significant life. Let your light shine.

I started the spring semester of 2020 with the intention of it being my last semester as an educator. The students I served during the spring semester of 2020 re-ignited hope and passion within me. My efforts to finish strong in what I thought was my last semester were met with such joy and belief that once again I fell in love with teaching.

I embraced the long-standing Nike slogan, "There is no finish line." I found the endurance to "keep on, keeping on." I hope in some small way this book will help you keep going and continue to fall in love with teaching over and over and over again.

"The universe is always speaking to us. Sending us little messages, causing coincidence and serendipities, reminding us to stop, to look around, to believe in something else, something more." – a quote copied into my journal, source unknown

THE FINAL WORDS

Early in my coaching career, just as I was developing the habit of keeping a journal, I wrote this: "One of the most difficult things that distance runners struggle with is staying motivated for the long haul. It's easy to be excited initially BUT it takes effort and time to remain motivated." This past summer my youngest daughter got married. In the days leading up to the wedding I borrowed a journal that I had kept for her as she grew (presented to her upon her high school graduation). A 2005 entry included a similar sentiment and speaks to the intense need within the teaching profession. "It is much easier to keep the fire burning than to rekindle it after it has gone out."

Writing short personal messages to someone I care deeply for is easy. I am constantly looking for reasons and opportunities to take on this meaningful task. Becoming the author of a book that serves to inspire and inform the teaching profession has taxed me tremendously. I have had to overcome several barriers to finish this imperfect text. The biggest of these barriers is the voice that comes, usually at night, and whispers that my work is unworthy. While far from perfect I hope you find it worthy. I have regularly felt a quiet, humble glory as I try to craft the words intended to bring hope and inspiration to the profession. I have opened my teaching practices, my heart, and the many journals I have kept throughout the four decades I filled the role of teacher. I have clung to the goals of TwE with no expectations of fame or fortune and I have finished the "race."

Writers are often told to write what they know. I don't know much BUT I know there are many amazing teachers out there that have endured the toughest of times and need some encouragement. I know there are early service teachers trying to navigate the tumultuous "waters" that exist in the profession that need a lifeline. This mission kept me going and brought me to this point. I can now release these words to the world in hopes of touching a few hearts and minds.

The first pages of this book include a personal letter to you, the reader. I am closing with a personal message from my old teacher's heart to your enduring teacher's heart. The teaching life is a journey, one that is more about the simple, unexpected moments we encounter along the way. This is where the real teaching happens.

Many years ago, on a warm September afternoon in Mt. Pleasant, Michigan the team I coached had just finished the first race of the season. Both teams had won so there were smiles, hugs, laughter all around. Even though some athletes had struggled a bit (the first race of a season can be a painful proving ground of preparation) the team shared a good feeling as they grabbed a drink, interacted with the opposing team, and readied for a cooldown. As I was moving towards that feel good circle, I noticed one of my female athletes rushing for the bus. Obviously distraught, this young lady had just competed in the first endurance race of her life. I hesitated. The easy choice would be to turn away from distress and join the team in our small celebration, guide them through the cooldown and provide a reminder of the importance for staying humble and hungry. The harder choice would be to follow a distraught young lady and try to "coach" her through the deep emotion that sometimes comes with intense physical pain. I made the harder choice and have spent a career making the harder choice again and again. As I entered the bus this athlete was alone and in tears. I joined her and was (painfully) privileged to hear her story. I mostly listened as she processed the hurt and past wounds of abandonment (she grew up fatherless). I couldn't remove her struggle, but I was able to "bind the wound" with a message of "it's going to be alright." In that moment I sensed I had made a small difference for her and a big difference for me. Noticing her attempt to escape and hide her pain permitted an opportunity for her to feel hopeful with a sense of belonging. This athlete never ran on the varsity team, but she became a significant and supportive part of a team that ended up tied for 2nd in the state finals. I learned a lesson that has remained a guiding light in my life.

Maya Angelou said, "The desire to reach for the stars is ambitious. The desire to reach hearts is wise." Be wise my teaching friends. Run your race with endurance.

ACKNOWLEDGEMENTS & REFERENCES

As mentioned earlier this book has been a work of heart and while it does contain some scholarly ideas, it mostly is a collection of ideas and stories based on my lived experience as a teacher who worked faithfully to build the kind of connections, with students and colleagues that added meaning to my work. I want to acknowledge that only with the help, support, and lasting relationships with other educators was I able to "finish the race." There are many teachers that I owe much gratitude, but I would like to share a list of committed and caring teachers that were instrumental in helping me complete this writing project that was a decade in the making. These special people gave their time and shared their hurts and hopes for the teaching profession. I am fortunate to have shared the journey with them.

Colorado: Michelle Hagerman, Taylor Breske, Craig Cerise, Rob Ames, Lance Betts, Ben Anderson, Danielle Lopez, Jennifer Magner, Derek Carlson

Wisconsin: Emma Polum, Jamie Schmitz, Jennifer Bowling, Erin Stoffel, Logan Taylor, Stephanie Weber, Loralee Curtin, Ralph Ramos, Jenna Simacek, Sara Ably, Katie Dombeck, Ben Quade

Michigan: Carrie Kunkle, Roberta Nista, Katie Butera, Tracey Jacobs, Matt Swanson

Oklahoma: Jason Proctor, Amy Brooks

Oregon: Doug Veysey

Wyoming: Scott Groenke

Montana: Hailey Hancock

Utah: Jack Harper

I offer a list of the resources I referenced in this book. All of these authors made me feel like I knew them intimately, even though I have only met them through their words (which are timeless). My teaching journey has been "rocky" but these authors provided me with someone to turn to when I needed insight and encouragement.

References

Andrews, A. (2009). *The Noticer.* Nashville, TN: Thomas Nelson

Barth, R. S. (2001). *Learning by heart.* San Francisco, CA: Jossey-Bass.

Bolman, L. G. & Deal, T. E. (2001). *Leading with soul: An uncommon journey of spirit.* San Francisco, CA: Jossey-Bass.

Brown, B. (2021). *Atlas of the Heart.* New York: Random House

Brown, B. (2018). *Dare to Lead.* London, England: Vermilion

Brown, B. (2012). *Daring Greatly.* New York: Gotham Books

Brown, B. (2010). *The Gifts of Imperfection.* Center City, MN: Hazelden Publishing

Brown, P. C. (2014). *Make it Stick: The Science of Successful Learning.* Cambridge, MA: The Belknap Press of Harvard University Press

Coelho, P. (1993). *The Alchemist.* New York: Harper One

Collins, J. (2001). *Good to Great.* London, England: Random House

Coutu, D. L. (2002). *How Resilience Works.* Harvard Business Review.

Coyle, D. (2018). *The Culture Code: The Secrets of Highly Successful Groups.* New York: Bantam Books

Deal, T. E. & Peterson, K. D. (2009). *Shaping School Culture: Pitfalls, Paradoxes, & Promises.* San Francisco, CA: Jossey-Bass

Dungy, T. (2010). *The Mentor Leader: Secrets to Building People and Teams that Win Consistently.* Carol Stream, IL: Tyndale House Publishers

Eldredge, J. (2022). *Resilient: Restoring Your Weary Soul in These Turbulent Times.* Nashville, TN: Nelson Books.

Eldredge, J. (2007). *Desire: The Journey We Must Take to Find the Life God offers*. Nashville, TN: Thomas Nelson, Inc.

Frankl, V. (1992). *Man's Search for Meaning*. Boston, MA: Beacon Press

Gladwell, M. (2013). *David and Goliath: Underdogs, Misfits, and the Art of Battling Giants*. New York: Little, Brown and Company

Hall, R. (2019). *Run the Mile You're In: Finding God in Every Step*. Grand Rapids, MI: Zondervan

Hargreaves, A. (2003). *Teaching in the knowledge society: Education in the age of insecurity*. New York: Teachers College Press.

Kahrs, B. (2011). *The Influence of Mentoring Relationships on Novice K-12 Teachers' Experiences* (Doctoral dissertation).

Kahrs, B. (2015). *It's Not About the Workouts: A Championship of the Soul*. Bloomington, IN: AuthorHouse

Lefstein, A. (2005). Thinking about the technical and the personal in teaching. *Cambridge Journal of Education, 35*(3), 333-356.

MacDonald, G. (1997). *Renewing Your Spiritual Passion*. Nashville, TN: Thomas Nelson

Marzano, R. & Lang-Raad, N. (2019). *The New Art and Science of Teaching: Mathematics*. Bloomington, IN: Solution Tree

McConaughey, M. (2020). *Greenlights*. New York: Crown

National Commission On Teaching And America's Future. (2007). *Building a 21st Century US Education System*. Washington, DC: Author.

Palmer, P. J. (2003). Teaching with heart and soul: Reflections on spirituality in teacher education. *Journal of Teacher Education*, 54(5), 376-385.

Palmer, P. J. (1998). *The courage to teach: Exploring the inner landscape of a teacher's life*. San Francisco, CA: Jossey-Bass.

Sergiovanni, T. J. (2005). *Strengthening the heartbeat: Leading and learning together in schools.* San Francisco, CA: Jossey-Bass.

Schon, D. A. (1983). *The Reflective Practitioner.* New York: Basic Books

The New Teacher Project (2015). *The Mirage: Confronting the Hard Truth About our Quest for Teacher Development.* Online publication: www.tntp.org

Wagner, T. & Dintersmith, T. (2015*). Most Likely to Succeed: Preparing Our Kids for the Innovation Era.* New York: Scribner

Wilkinson, B. (1992). *The Seven Laws of the Learner: How to Teach Almost Anything to Practically Anyone.* Sisters, Oregon: Multnomah Publishers

ABOUT THE AUTHOR

The author, Dr. Brad Kahrs, is a lifelong educator. His four decades in the teaching profession includes 27 years in k-12 education where he served in the roles of math instructor, coach, and mentor. His 12 years in Higher Education focused on creating quality experiences for beginning teachers. On the heels of the completion of this writing project he continues to support the lives of many teachers in several states and searches for the answer to the question "what's next?" He resides in Murray, Utah with his wife of 43 years where he consistently seeks adventure, beauty, and challenge, often in the nearby Wasatch Mountains. Feel free to reach out for a conversation or message of hope and inspiration by emailing Dr. Kahrs at: bradleyjkahrs@gmail.com

Printed in the United States
by Baker & Taylor Publisher Services